G000038874

SPIRIT OF NATURE
POETRY OF THE EARTH

PHOTOGRAPHIC SKETCHES
OF DEVON

SPIRIT OF NATURE

POETRY OF THE EARTH

PHOTOGRAPHIC SKETCHES
OF DEVON

ROGER POLLEY • JOHN WOODMAN

DEVON BOOKS

First published in Great Britain 1994 by Devon Books

British Library Cataloguing in Publication Data.
Data for this publication is available from the British Library.

ISBN 0 86114 890 8

Published with the support of:

The Countryside Commission
Devon County Council (Environment Committee)
The University of Plymouth

DEVON BOOKS
Official Publisher to Devon County Council
Halsgrove House
Lower Moor Way
Tiverton, Devon EX16 6SS
Tel: 0884 243242
Fax:0884 243325

Designed for Devon Books by Topics Visual Information, Exeter.
Printed and bound in Great Britain by BPC Wheatons Ltd.

FOREWORD

BY RICHARD MABEY

In 1847, Joseph John made a remarkable and famous picture of a fragment of virgin Czechoslovakian forest. It is a precise plan of an exact plot, showing all the trees, live and dead, in their places. But what is most compelling about it is the way it weaves together time and space. The fallen trees have length and taper and angle. They are piled up on each other, like spillikins, some lying under, some over their neighbours. A few have blurred, decaying ends, standing out against the abruptly snapped tops of others, memorials to different kinds of dissolution. By contrast, the standing timber is a mere scatter of dots and circles, barely real dyed-in-the-grain trees yet.

The mapping has been regularly repeated on the same plot ever since, and has produced a unique slow-motion record, a time-lapse almost, of the evolution of natural woodland, and of the way that natural catastrophe and regeneration always sit side by side in living systems.

I was reminded of John's historic record when I saw Roger Polley's and John Woodman's photographic responses to Devon County Council's Environmental Land Management Scheme (ELMS), which supported imaginative projects in the countyside that will benefit both the land and local people. There is the same commitment to intricacy and detail, the same conviction that anodyne terms like 'timeless' and 'changeless' do no justice to the vitality of nature. In Polley and Woodman's composite pictures, continuity and change, seasonal shift and human work, run together just as they do in nature. In an ancient orchard a tangled close-up of mazy twigs forms a frieze, or hedge, for the portraits of the fruit trees and apples, which have themselves been pruned and cut. A series of studies of a lake edge are fractured and reconstructed, as if they had been flooded. The light streaming through thinned trees *contains* the logs it will eventually help create.

Joseph John's maps proved to be a crucial resource, a scientific record which was also an intriguing work of art. Polley and Woodman's *Spirit of Nature: Poetry of the Earth*, the collective expressions of landholders, artists, poets, planners and map-makers, is a work of the imagination which is also a vital piece of science, a body of evidence of the links between all creatures in the commonwealth of nature.

DEVON COUNTY COUNCIL'S

ENVIRONMENTAL LAND MANAGEMENT SCHEME

New recreational opportunities, wildlife conservation, landscape enhancement and the preservation of historic features are all things which have been achieved through Devon County Council's Environmental Land Management Scheme (ELMS). ELMS is a pioneering project which relies on a partnership between landowners and Devon County Council. The partnership, which is normally for ten years, involves the County Council providing financial assistance and the landowner providing the land and practical management.

ELMS was launched by the County Council in April 1990 following a suggestion by the Country Landowners Association in their report 'Enterprise in the Rural Enviroment'. Since the launch 100 partnerships have been signed. On the ground this means that 1275 acres of land are managed for wildlife and landscape enhancement and 45 miles of new paths and trails have been created.

In the first two years emphasis was given to the conservation of culm grassland. Such grassland, which is found in small pockets on the Culm Measures of North Devon, has never been ploughed, drained or fertilised and is consequently very rich in wildflowers and unusual sedges and grasses. In the spring culm grassland is often carpeted in pink orchids.

As new grant schemes became available to conserve culm grassland, particularly the Countryside Commission's Countryside Stewardship Scheme, ELMS changed its emphasis towards the provision of trails. Twenty-five farm, forest and nature trails have been established enabling individuals and specialist interest groups to explore corners of Devon which would otherwise be hidden. Some of the gems which can be seen include semi-natural woodland, culm grassland, medieval fish ponds and historic follies. From many hilltops stunning views across rolling countryside are revealed. Where possible these 'gems' have been made accessible to the less mobile. Surfaced paths have been laid and in some places sensory gardens and raised flower beds have been created. New links in the existing road and path network have also been made and recently some ELMS partnerships have been for the creation of cycle ways.

With such a variety of things to look at and enjoy, John Woodman and Roger Polley saw ELMS as an exciting theme for their work. With financial assistance from Devon County Council they spent twelve months travelling the County, photographing what they saw, talking to the landowners and putting together their photomontages. Just as John and Roger prepared for the launch of this publication, ELMS celebrated the completion of its hundredth scheme.

CATHY FITZROY
COUNTRYSIDE GRANTS CO-ORDINATOR
ENVIRONMENT DEPARTMENT, DEVON COUNTY COUNCIL

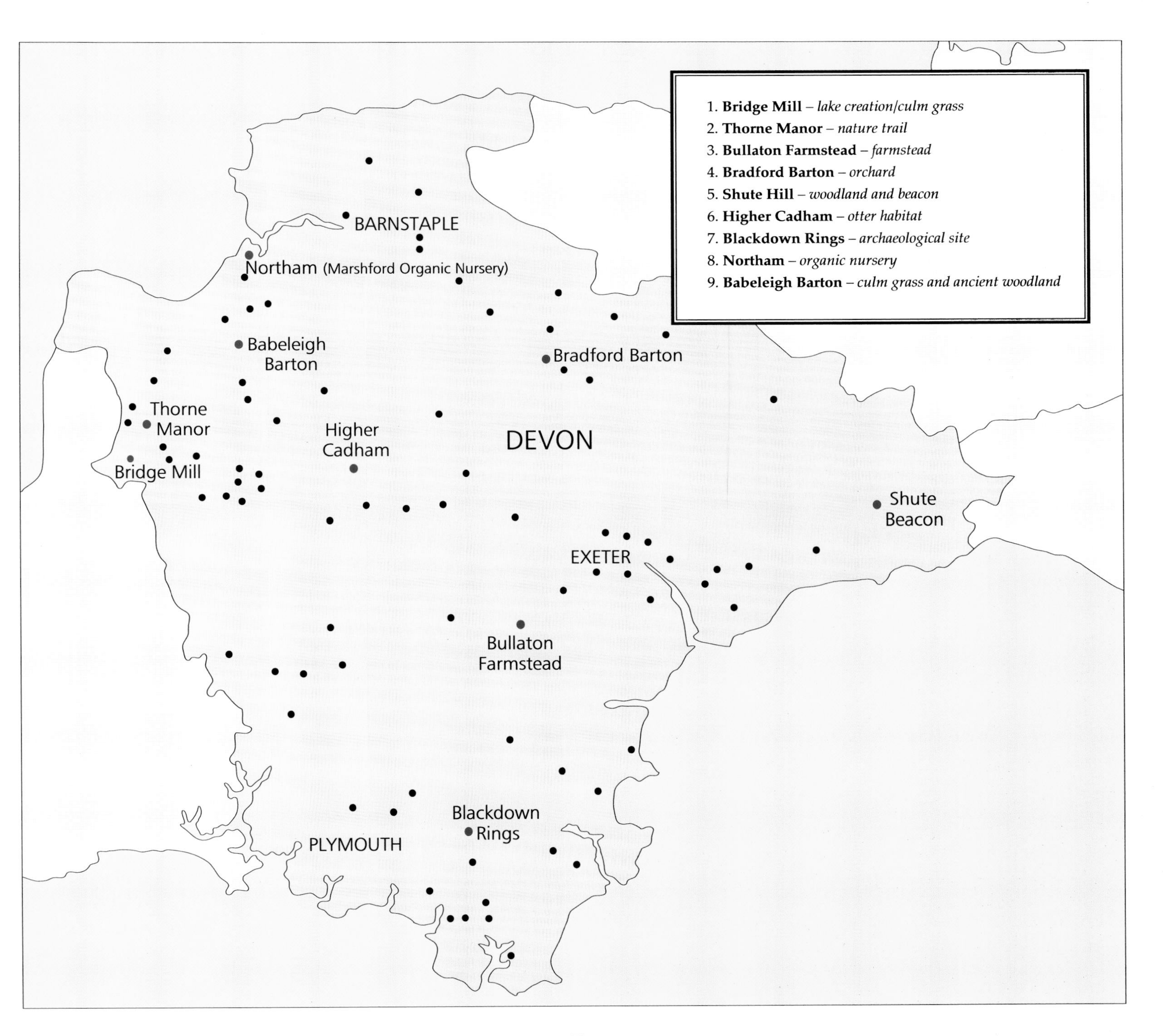
1. **Bridge Mill** – *lake creation/culm grass*
2. **Thorne Manor** – *nature trail*
3. **Bullaton Farmstead** – *farmstead*
4. **Bradford Barton** – *orchard*
5. **Shute Hill** – *woodland and beacon*
6. **Higher Cadham** – *otter habitat*
7. **Blackdown Rings** – *archaeological site*
8. **Northam** – *organic nursery*
9. **Babeleigh Barton** – *culm grass and ancient woodland*
BARNSTAPLE
Northam (Marshford Organic Nursery)
Babeleigh Barton
Bradford Barton
Thorne Manor
Higher Cadham
DEVON
Bridge Mill
Shute Beacon
EXETER
Bullaton Farmstead
Blackdown Rings
PLYMOUTH

PREFACE

'Collaboration'

Artists and designers have taken much creative inspiration from the landscape and stimulated a public fascination with the picturesque qualities of nature. It has promoted a well-established romantic association with rural Britain which does much to encourage the tourist visitor to Devon. Working from this tradition this project adds a new dimension through its patient system of recording and assemblage. It puts forward new methods of interpretation and draws attention to the importance of the values embodied in the everyday and ordinary locations.

Working within the objectives and terms of reference set down by the ELMS scheme has enabled the artistic investigations of those coordinating the project to be directly associated with the work of professionals and campaigners from other interested disciplines. It is anticipated that through its visual interpretation of landscape the project will lead to a more imaginative and informed response to the use and management of the rural environment.

The outcome of the photographic research project presented as an exhibition and publication comes from the vision and determination of the Project Directors, John Woodman and Roger Polley, and the constructive support provided by the University of Plymouth, Devon County Council and the Countryside Commission. Without this collaboration the project could not have been realised, and everyone would have been the loser.

PROFESSOR DAVID JEREMIAH
UNIVERSITY OF PLYMOUTH

CONTENTS

'DEVON IS!'

Devon is Alphington, Ashcombe, Ashwater, Beer, Beaford, Berry Pomeroy, Bishopsteignton, Bow, Broadwoodwidger, Berrynarbor, Cheriton Fitzpaine, Clannaborough, Clovelly, Dunchideock, Eggesford, and the list goes on through more than 400 parishes to Upottery, Virginstow, Woolfardisworthy, Woolfardisworthy (yes, there are two of them!), Yarcombe, Yealmpton and Zeal Monachorum.

Each parish is unique and distinct but they are all united by history, themes, threads and colours. Their residents can tell you about these matters, those corners, those issues and the folklore and culture that makes each parish and each part of that parish special to them. It may be folk knowledge about the Roman origin of a particular place only recently confirmed from a scientific point of view by aerial archaeology. It may be the history of the church, the school, its bridges or its nature. Equally it could be its bypass, its former traffic jams or its locally brewed beer. Devon to the local resident, the 'local', the Devonian, is not neccessarily the same Devon as that of the visitor or the recent 'incomer'. Martyn Brown in his *Red Guide – Devon* (1989) provides an interesting insight into visitor perception. He suggests that:

> *The most popular image of Devon as a holiday destination is epitomised in the promotion of Torbay as the English Riviera; posters create an image of a sub-tropical paradise with perpetually blue skies and apparently warm seas but the image masks the tranquillity and charm of much of the County and belies its rich variety.*
>
> *A contrasting view of the County might emphasise the fiery red soils of south-east Devon, matching the herds of Devon Red cattle, cider from a stoneware flask in an orchard of trees bent low under the heavy crop of fruit; black faced shaggy sheep seeking the shelter of roadside ditches; hedges plastered in primroses; and winters of deep snow that cut off farms for days on end.*

These views are some way away from those of the idyllic photogenic paradise of the sepia photographs which were a feature of railway compartments and waiting rooms of the Great Western Railway. United by proximity to GWR stations these former images form a theme which can still be detected in Devon even where Beeching's infamous axe struck.

But how can a picture of 'real' Devon be presented? Geology and climate together with their resultant colours and light provide one thread; history, culture and folklore another; whilst a third is the unconformity created by contrasts between neighbouring settlements despite their similar origin or modern day function.

Throughout Europe geology and its related topography help to define a sense of place. Geology not only creates landscape and its related wildlife habitats but more importantly it provides the local building materials. Its influence on soils and vegetation has historically determined the way in which an area is formed although today the Common Agriculture Policy appears to have taken on this role with the countryside changing colours by turn from green, to yellow and to purple at the command of some cosmic artistic conductor far away from Devon.

Devon has a special place in the science of geology. Not only is it the site of at least one field trip for every UK geology student but it is the only county which gives its name to a geological era. The 'Devonian' system was defined in 1839 by the Reverend Adam Sedgewick and Sir Robert Murchison for those strata deposited after the Silurian slates and the limestones of Wales and before the coal bearing strata of the Midlands.

Devon's geology is responsible for the County's characteristic red soils and red sea cliffs. Although the red rocks of Devon cover a considerable part of the County, this is still only a part of the whole. The characteristic 'red' image probably arises from railway routes into the County and along the coast in the Dawlish/Teignmouth area.

The tors of the granite heartland, the slates, gritstones, limestones, pebble beds and chalks all help to define what Devon is. Each of these has been exploited by local residents over hundreds of years to create a complexity of building styles and materials. Devon buildings look and feel distinctively Devonian because of their use of local Devon materials, and of their plan forms and decorative details which were adopted to suit local conditions. No one building of the period 1400 to 1800 is exactly the same as another.

One of the most interesting building materials is cob. Cob is simply the Devon word for a mud wall. No other county in England has as much mud walling as Devon! Cob was used as the traditional means of mass wall construction throughout most of rural Devon during the period of the fourteenth to the nineteenth centuries.

The basic material was the on-site sub-soil. The cob was prepared by adding straw to the sub-soil, and the mixing process was often achieved by the treading of cattle whose dung provided a 'plasticiser' for the mixture. Cob itself varies from place to place as a result of local traditions and the widely differing nature of local sub-soils.

Devon's history has been influenced not just by its geology but also by its geographical place in the world. Whilst its parishes are all distinctly different, to a large extent they have a common history and ancestry. Thought by some residents to be the most south-westerly county, as the land beyond the Tamar defines itself as another country, Devon has no neighbours to the north and south except the Bristol and the English Channels and is bounded to the east by the high ground of Exmoor and the Blackdowns.

Its situation has led to its fishing and international trading traditions. It has a long history of trading with North America, Northern Europe, the Iberian Peninsula and the Mediterranean. The farming, shipbuilding, quarrying and naval traditions which account for large parts of the population for many hundreds of years stem from Devon's peripheral but international position.

This history has created much of that which is most valued and distinctive in Devon today. This is a both a rural and urban feature of the County. It is interesting to contrast adjacent towns and villages, Totnes and Newton Abbot in the south of the County, and Topsham and Starcross located on opposite sides of the Exe estuary. Totnes and Newton Abbot are both market towns, lying at the heads of tidal river systems and are settlements of considerable history. Although both have their medieval origins, Totnes developed within its defensive walls whilst Newton Abbot was born of the amalgamation of two manorial boroughs. Both are railway towns, but whilst Totnes station serves the town with little impact on its development, Newton Abbot developed as a significant railway junction town. The railway set the foundations for the blossoming of Newton with the construction of a number of Victorian buildings and squares. Totnes has retained its medieval character and is now a centre for 'alternative cultures'.

Superficially Topsham and Starcross share many common characteristics – once small settlements on the Exe estuary, with a strong relationship with the river and linear development patterns.

Their history and buildings, however, reveal contrasting origins. Topsham goes back to Roman times with much development taking place in the sixteenth to eighteenth centuries. It retains its many small streets and alleys, and in the Strand are to be found the attractive 'Dutch' houses built in the early 1700s by the wool merchants. Dutch bricks were brought back from Holland as ballast and the design of the houses was clearly influenced by the Holland connection.

Starcross has humbler origins in the sixteenth century as a collection of fishermen's cottages. Brunel's atmospheric railway dominated the waterfront in the nineteenth century although a number of architecturally interesting buildings were constructed about the same time.

These contrasts, this history, these themes, make it clear that in carrying out its statutory duties the County Council cannot properly maintain its stewardship of Devon without giving them proper recognition. A key role in this is played by the County Environment Department (logo – a Lucombe Oak), a multi-disciplinary department employing *inter alia* planners, engineers, ecologists, environmentalists, archaeologists, mathematicians, modellers, computer wizards, traffic specialists and listed building experts. Its responsibilities include the largest road network of any English county by far, planning, waste regulation, country parks, the environment, traffic and recycling. Its recently published Directory of Services details some 77 different services.

As an integrated department, the protection and enhancement of both the rural and urban environment is a prime function. The County Council's pioneering ELMS initiative has played a key part in this approach.

EDWARD CHORLTON
COUNTY ENVIRONMENT DIRECTOR
DEVON COUNTY COUNCIL

NOTE: This is an edited version of a paper presented at Common Ground's National Conference on Local Distinctiveness in September 1993 and published in *Local Distinctiveness*, Common Ground (1993).

CELEBRATING THE LANDSCAPE

Landscape has long been an established genre of the arts in China and Japan where themes, such as seasons and elements have held a spiritual significance. European landscape art however, has a relatively brief history; it did not even become an independent genre until the seventeenth century. Nature though, has been depicted universally by man throughout the ages, ever since the first prehistoric cave paintings, its portrayal originating in humanity's complex relationship to the world. Nature is, of course, a construct and as such, is constantly changing and affected by our perception and our interaction with the Universe. Our culture, religion and science have mostly defined nature as something quite separate from ourselves – nature as an independent reality – fortunately many artists conceive nature quite differently.

According to the *Oxford English Dictionary* the use of the word landscape was first recorded in 1603 and meant 'a picture representing natural inland scenery'. Today apart from meaning the artistic genre of landscape, we use the word in a much wider sense to mean: land, scenery, place, terrain, territory, countryside and topography. Early photographers quickly realised that the photographic medium excelled in an exact and believable depiction of place. Artists who claimed to portray realistically the Wild West yet had never set foot in North America, filled their landscape paintings with alien European vegetation and topography. The photographer unlike the artist had to be present in the landscape to make the picture.

Being present at the photographic location is something that Roger Polly and John Woodman make into a ceremony. Or as they call it a 'celebration'. Their works take time. Not just 1/125th of a second or even a second, but hours and days are spent in observing the changes that are taking place before them, around them and within themselves. Sometimes they return again and again to the same location to record the transformations that have taken place with the shifting of the seasons.

We live at a time when there are no areas of the globe that are uncharted, that are not crossed by radio, or television waves, or that are unaffected by pollution in one form or another. Jets cross the sky and satellites circle the Earth. Nuclear warheads can cross continents in minutes. Yet we still live with a romantic ideal, a notion of wilderness – a place untouched by the hand of man, where we can get away from it all and be close to nature.

Until quite recently, the 'unsightly' human presence of industrial man, pylons, factories, motorways, etc. had been unacknowledged, unseen and avoided, in landscape. It is after all a modern phenomena, which has not been encompassed in the ideal landscape. The heritage of the ideal also lives on in the advertising photograph, where the image is exploited in countless campaigns selling everything from cigarettes to cars, depicts an untouched, unspoilt and beautiful view. When *National Geographic* magazine 'moved' by digital means, one of the Great Pyramids of Egypt, in order that it might fit better on its cover, it became clear that the only ideal landscape might one day exist in a computer. Industrial man first raped the Earth and then wants her as a pin-up.

In this work Polley and Woodman have photographed in the countryside of Devon. City dwellers can easily romanticise its scenic beauty, but much of its beauty to man lies in the age old care that previous generations of farmers have devoted to its existence. The countryside was once cared for like a garden, sadly today it needs protection from industrial exploitation and the harsh farming methods of modern agriculture, where chemicals and heavy machinery have given efficiency at a huge cost to wildlife and the very features that we normally associate with the landscape, such as copses, hedgerows and small streams.

Polley and Woodman's photographs consist of panoramas and close ups. There are changes in scale and sometimes complete seasons of references, assembled in multi-images, consisting of often 30 to 40 prints. The grouping of these build a whole within one frame. Some works occasionally verge on abstraction, but are nevertheless recognisable for what they represent.

They are equally involved and are present in all stages of the work. Even their technique itself is quite democratic. The colour prints which they assemble, are the same size as those used in the family album.

By choosing to exhibit their projects in the same region as they are photographed, an immediate relationship between the viewer, the work which is presented, and the local environment itself, is created. This relationship helps strengthen the ultimate and crucial aim of their work, which is quite simply to make us care for the world around us.

The freshness of seeing familiar rural countryside areas depicted in this colourful yet contemplative and studious way, can aid in preserving the land's value as a source of inspiration and well being for us all. We must learn to see, love and care for the beauty, of not just the more unpopulated wilderness, or the majesty of the National Parks, but of the landscape much nearer home where most of us live. Finally we must learn that we are a part of nature and the Earth and must cherish all the gentle relationships between humanity and the land that we can, if our species is to survive.

John S. Webb

SEASONS

Spring is a time of hope and rejoicing, in every heart there is song, conscious or unconscious. It is the season of love, beauty, and wonder, when earth becomes heaven. Nothing is impossible, nothing beyond belief when man sees for himself the miracle which spring shows when seed, bulb, bare twig, dried root are transformed into flower, leaf, and tree with all the wealth of colour, fragrance, shape and beauty, which make the earth a garden.

The sound, the sight and fragrance of this season give something that is indescribable. The variety of green is in itself a wonder, and shows the infinite creative capacity of the earth.

I sometimes ask myself which leaf I think the most beautiful. I can never decide between the fresh green of the young beech, the quivering sensitiveness of the birch, or the richness of the oak. And then I think of the elm, the chestnut, the hawthorn. Every tree and every bush has its own particular beauty. And to feel the softness of the leaves against my face is a caress of marvellous refreshment.

Spring presents us with hope, showing us the result of persistence, continuance, effort, and endurance.

The countryside is drenched with fragrance. In summer we count the lovely month of June when the soft air fondles leaf and grass blade. Larks are easing their hearts above our heads in cascades of song, blackbirds are clamorous, wings are about us occupied with important business. There is the golden gorse, the wood and meadow knows sun and shade, there is blue distance, the gold of buttercups and the silver of moon daisies under the bright stars.

The hedge, the wood, the marsh, the hillside and the garden are aglow with colour and abound in fragrance.

Spring is the youth of the year; summer, its rich maturity. There is a generous giving about this season; a richness, a bestowal. It is as though Nature gives us a sacrament of beauty in the fullness of its life.

Autumn sings the swan-song of the year, the scents she bestows linger as though they desire to be held in remembrance.

To many this season is the most beautiful, certainly the earth's richest – the harvest of the year. The life-blood of all growing things is being spilt; it is the communion service of the earth – take it and be thankful. These are the words I read on every bush, tree, and hedgerow, in the garden, on the moor and marsh.

Autumn bestows all her rich store as she passes and with this passing she gives a sense of fulfilment none of her sisters achieve – she comes full circle. There are few that remain unmoved as they watch her splendid pageant, her last effort of flaming life before the surrender.

Autumn gives the glad thought that beauty cannot die as long as the world endures, that it is not something only to be presently enjoyed but to be stored and treasured.

Now the trees stand clear against the sky, showing their intricate tracery of branch and twig. Winter gives an X-ray picture of tree and bush... at this season the earth suffers bombardment – hammering hail, bitter frost and driving north wind – yet in spite of all this she remains unperturbed; occupied with construction, she is conscious of conception; miracles are in preparation. The multitudinous forces of the underworld are active in preparation for the birth of winter's daughter.

Bring your magic and transform with your fairy fingers
Every twig, bush, hedge and tree,
And the grim town with it slum and factory.
Cover them with all your fairy feathers
And sprinkle the earth with your diamond dust.

NANCY PRICE

BRIDGE MILL

We moved to our Bridgerule smallholding in 1987, with the intention of farming our 16 acres organically alongside positive management to benefit wildlife. A 4.5 acre field beside the River Tamar had a low-lying marshy central area and in time of flood the river water filled this hollow to give the illusion of a lake. With no sizeable stillwater in the locality, this illusion was crying out to be made into a permanent feature of our landscape.

As part of the support provided through the Devon ELMS project, a trial pond was dug and left for twelve months to prove adequate water levels through the seasons. With this achieved, the lake construction was carefully planned to follow the natural contours of the land, mimicking the area usually flooded. A range of depths and slopes were incorporated to provide diversity of habitat for a broad range of wildlife. I worked hard alongside the contractor's swing shovels with my old tractor and trailer, or with shovel and cement mixer, as the earthmoving took place; and there was more hard work afterwards building fences, hanging gates, planting trees and hedges.

Before the lake was finished the wildlife had begun to move in. Wild duck would flight in at dusk, and rise into the morning sky as we entered the field at the start of another day's work. Snipe fed along the margins, patterning the soft mud with their footprints. The day that the channel between the two islands was dug, a brilliant blue dragonfly (the broad bodied chaser) was hawking up and down the narrow ribbon of water we had just created. Once the lake had filled, plants began to colonise the margins; some had grown on the site beforehand, some we planted or introduced as seed; many simply arrived by themselves. Insects, amphibians and birds arrived, flying, walking, creeping, hopping. Fish stocks were introduced eighteen months on. The whole process of colonisation was fascinating to watch, unfolding day by day, and we kept a diary to record it.

Now, three years on, the lake increasingly looks an integral part of the landscape, and supports an astonishing variety of life. There is tangible benefit to the locality as visiting or breeding wildlife spreads out into the surrounding area, while open days and school visits enable others to share our enjoyment. Most days I walk around the lake, alert for anything new or unusual – but sometimes to sit quietly on the bank near dawn or dusk is most rewarding of all; then it is that the tranquil atmosphere of the waterside can be best appreciated. When we look upon the beauty of the setting, and the growing richness of the wildlife, we feel great pleasure in knowing that we have helped to make it all happen.

ALAN BEAT

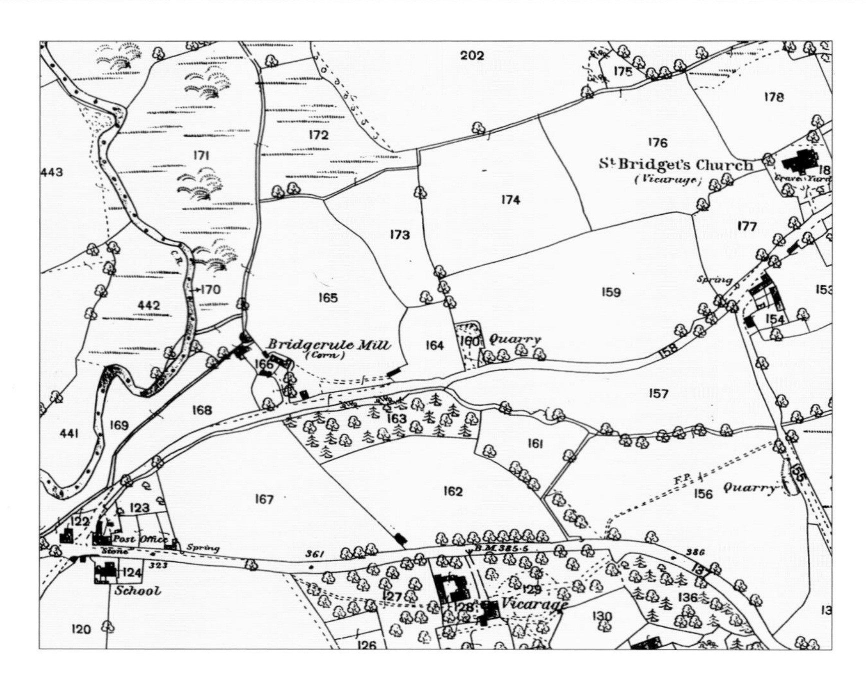

202
175
178
171
172
176
443
St Bridget's Church
(Vicarage)
174
173
177
Spring
159
442
170
165
Bridgerule Mill
(Corn)
164
160
Quarry
154
166
157
158
163
168
441
169
161
167
162
156
Quarry
123
122
Post Office
Stone
Spring
361
124
School
323
129
Vicarage
127
128
130
136
386
120
126

EXTRACTS FROM THE LAKE DIARY

1990

20TH AUGUST	*The diggers start work*
12TH SEPTEMBER	*Construction work finished*
15TH SEPTEMBER	*Grey heron hunting the margins*
19TH SEPTEMBER	*Water level rising after rain*
27TH SEPTEMBER	*Level steady at 15″ on marker post. Pied and grey wagtails, snipe, also green sandpipers*
2ND OCTOBER	*Level now 33″, starting to flood the shallow bay*
7TH OCTOBER	*Grey heron at first light. Level 51″*
16TH OCTOBER	*Lake full at 66″ and running from outflow*
25TH OCTOBER	*Dabchick on the water*
6TH NOVEMBER	*Planted seeds of yellow flag iris around margins, also plants of bogbean, yellow loosestrife, greater spearwort, hornwort and water mint. Snipe and fieldfares seen.*
24TH NOVEMBER	*River flooding after heavy overnight rain, banks holding it back from the lake as planned.*

1991

FEBRUARY	*Frozen over during cold spell. Dusting of snow on the ice showed fox tracks.*
11TH MARCH	*Pair of Canada geese stayed all day.*
12TH MARCH	*Planted islands and margin of shallow bay with various native trees and shrubs – spindle, crab apple, wild pear, dogwood, blackthorn, hazel and willow.*
13TH MARCH	*Lots of frog spawn hatching, toads busy laying.*
17TH APRIL	*Mallard duck with chicks by flood bank, fox at the shallow bay. Swallows active over water.*
1ST MAY	*Bridgerule playgroup visit.*
14TH MAY	*Bridgerule school visit to pond-dip.*
20TH MAY	*Sand martins and swallows active, cuckoo overflying. Vigorous growth of starwort over lake bed.*
30TH MAY	*First 'open evening' walk around lake, about 40 people attending. Young frogs emerging at margins.*
16TH JULY	*Looked at dragonflies, identified: common blue, blue-tailed, scarce blue-tailed and white-legged damselflies; also common darter, broad-bodied chaser, banded demoiselle.*
26TH JULY	*Swimming in the lake, Katie found a moorhen's nest on the little island holding 5 eggs.*
20TH SEPTEMBER	*Juvenile cormorant on the water.*
DECEMBER	*Frozen over for a few days. Fox seen playing on the ice at 9am in bright sunshine.*

1992

20th January	*Planted pendulous sedge around margin, also several sallow cuttings. Snipe and one mallard flushed.*
25th February	*Looked at water plants from the boat – established stands of curly pondweed, stonewort and starwort.*
8th March	*100 lbs of mirror and common carp stocked, average size about 1lb each.*
19th April	*Remains of two eaten carp found*
27th April	*Fresh remains of carp found on large island – fins and scales. Female sparrowhawk at dusk.*
5th May	*No signs of fish killed for some days. Moorhen's nest on small island with 8 eggs.*
5th June	*Holsworthy school day visit.*
25th June	*Putford school day visit.*
31st July	*More dragonflies identified: Emperor and golden-ringed dragonflies; azure and emerald damselflies.*
20th August	*100 small tench stocked, 4-6" fish.*
17th September	*4 grey herons fishing this morning.*
14th December	*2 fresh fish kills (carp) on bankside grass.*
27th December	*Rowed across to island, found six kills plus spraints and footprints of otter.*

1993

9th January	*Completed twin-strand electric fence around flood bank and switched on, hoping to deter otter*
17th January	*No further evidence of otter found so far. Lots of frogspawn in margins*
10th April	*Canada goose sitting on small island. Still no signs of otter*
10th May	*Moorhen's nest with 6 eggs in marginal reeds. Single gosling seen swimming, also mallard with 7 chicks.*
6th June	*Geese have left after losing their gosling. No trace found, but 2 unhatched eggs left. One fish kill found on small island (otter)*
30th June	*2 freshly-killed mallard ducklings found on islands* (mink?). *Pond dipping with Putford school produced lots of insect life plus newt larvae in large numbers.*
4th July	*Fished for a few hours, caught one mirror carp of 4.5lbs*
29th July	*Two otters seen in river alongside lake, mother and well-grown cub. Moving upstream, pausing to rest and preen, playing together in water.*
21st September	*Watched kingfisher fishing in lake; green sandpiper on passage.*
23 September	*Broad-leaved pondweed now established in small clump between islands. Common darters egglaying.*
21 November	*Lake frozen over in very cold spell*
4 December	*Carp remains found by far bay – otter again*

1994

3 January	*Barn owl at dusk, hunting over lakeside*
12 January	*Checked islands and margins carefully, found three recent otter kills*
29 January	*Three mallard on large island, perhaps a dozen snipe around margins. Geese heard flighting in a dusk*
30 January	*Third stocking of carp introduced, fully scaled common carp up to 8lbs each*
31 January	*8lb common carp killed and half eaten by otter. Extended electric fence around entire perimeter of lake*
19 February	*Two more otter kills found, including another 8lb carp*
5 March	*Completed construction of 400 metre permanent wire mesh fence to exclude otters – a reluctant move which has to be faced if a breeding stock of fish is to establish itself.*
20 March	*Pair of Canada geese here daily. Nest scrape on small island, same place as last year*
6 April	*Female goose now sitting*
15 April	*First swallows seen over water*
24 April	*Grasshopper warbler singing along the mill leat. Goose still sitting. No fish lost since fence completed, although fresh tracks along river margin show otters are close by.*
6 May	*Four little gosling seen on the water with their parents*
12 May	*Still four goslings surviving. Two unhatched eggs in nestscrape on small island- infertile?*

Alan Beat

This leaning tree with ivy overhung
This crooked brook oer which is rudely flung
A slender plank that bends beneath the feet
And that small hill the shepherds summer seat
Make up a picture to the mind and wear
A nobler gild than pallace walls can heir
To me the wild wind dashes oer the scene
Enchantments shades of vivifying green
I see her sketchy pensil in her hand
Painting the moving scene to fairey land
The black birds music from the hazel bower
Turns into golden drops this summer shower
To think the rain that wets his sutty wing
Should wake the gushes of his soul to sing
Hark at the melody how rich and loud
Like daylight breaking through the morning cloud
How luscious through that sea of green it floats
Knowest thou of music breathed from sweeter notes
Than that wild minstrel of the summer shower
Breathes at this moment from that hazel bower
To me the anthem of a thousand tongues
Were poor and idle to the simple songs
To that high toned and edifying bird
That sings to nature by itself unheard

2

There is a language wrote on earth and sky
By Gods own pen in silent majesty
There is a voice thats heard and felt and seen
In springs young shades and summers endless green
There is a book of poesy and spells
In which that voice in sunny splendour dwells
There is a page in which that voice aloud
Speakst music to the few and not the crowd
Though no romantic scenes my feet hath trod
The voice of nature as the voice of God
Appeals to me in every tree and flower
Breathing his glory magnitude and power
In natures open book I read and see
Beautys rich lesson in this seeming pea
Crowds see no magic in the trifling thing
Pshaw tis a weed and millions came with spring
I hear rich music where so eer I look
But heedless worldlings chide the brawling brook
And that small lark between me and the sky
Breaths sweetest strains of mornings melody
Yet by the heedless crowd tis only heard
As the small warbling of a common bird
That oer the plough teams hails the morning sun
They see no music from such majic won
Yet I see melody in natures laws
Or do I dream still wonder bids me pause
I pause and hear a voice that speaks aloud
Tis not on earth nor in the thunder cloud
The many look for sound tis silence speaks
And song like sunshine from her rapture breaks
I hear it in my bosom ever near
Tis in these winds and they are everywhere
It casts around my vision majic spells
And makes earth heaven where poor fancy dwells
I read its language and its speech is joy
So without teaching when a lonely boy

3

Each weed to me did happy tidings bring
Plain as the daisey wrote the name of spring
And Gods own language unto nature given
Seemed universal as the light of heaven
And common as the grass upon the plain
That all may read and meet with joy again
Save the unheeding heart who like the tomb
Shuts joy in darkness and forbids its bloom

JOHN CLARE

THORNE MANOR

Our nature trail which also includes a stretch of the tow-path beside the disused Bude Canal is approximately one mile long and came about because of our childrens' interest in wildlife. Various habitats have been encouraged, including wet meadowland, heathland and rough pasture, hedges, mixed woodland and a lake.

The trail starts at the medieval chapel (c. 1377) and runs down the old farm lane into the reserve. None of the fields within the reserve have been treated with artificial sprays or fertilisers in living memory and thus provide a unique haven for plants and insects. Close by are medieval fish ponds now cleared under support from the Devon ELMS scheme.

The Lake has been excavated and both mallard and teal are regular visitors; the bullrush (or reedmace) and bur reed have established themselves. Bur reed was once believed to be an antidote to snake venom. The shrubs and trees in this area encourage some of the smaller birds, including reed warbler, bullfinch, chiff-chaff and tits. While in the fields the buzzard can be seen soaring above the valley, and closer to the woodland may be glimpsed a sparrowhawk.

The woodland surrounding the canal provides a variety of habitat and levels of canopy cover. Fallen and dead branches are important in providing a suitable habitat for various fungi and insects.

On entering the woodland the trees are thickly draped with lichens, the most common being lungwort. There are some five hundred British species of lichen which grow on trees and shrubs, although few have common names. The presence of lichen is a good indication as to the absence of air pollution, as these are sensitive plants with no root system.

CHARLES CLARKE

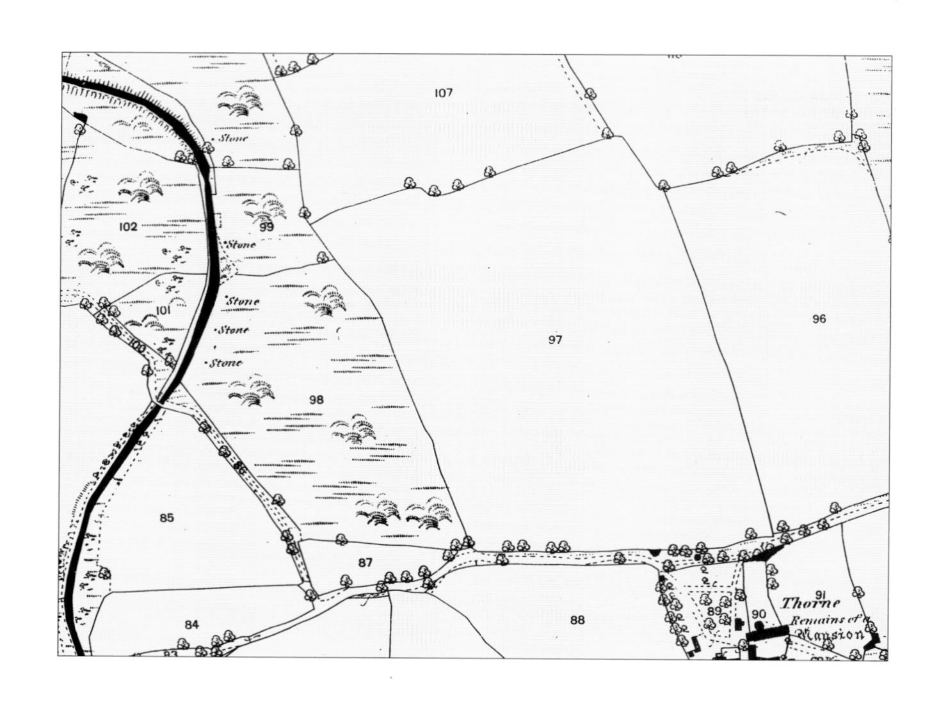
107
Stone
102
99
Stone
Stone
101
Stone
Stone
100
97
96
98
85
87
84
88
89
90
91
Thorne
Remains of a
Mansion

In some mysterious way woods have never seemed to me to be static things.
In physical terms, I move through them; yet in metaphysical ones,
they seem to move through me.

John Fowles

I see now what I like best about the green density,
the unpeopled secrecy of the Devon countryside
that the chance history gave me was its explorability.
At a time I thought I was learning to shoot
and fish (also to trespass and poach I'm afraid)
to botanize and birdwatch; but I was really addicting
myself, and beyond curability, to the pleasures of discovery,
and in particular of isolated discovery and experience.
The lonelier the place, the better it pleased me; its silence,
its aura, its peculiar conformation its enclosedness.

We enter. The place has an intense stillness, as if here the
plant side of creation rules and even birds are banned;
parts of older trees are dead and decayed,
crumbling into humus, they carry their huge sleeves
of ferns and other plants. But in its silence, the waitingness
of the place, that is so haunting; a quality all woods will have
on occasion, but which is overwhelming here – a drama,
but of a time-span humanity cannot conceive.
A pastness, a presentness, a skill with tenses
the writer in me knows he will never know;
partly out of his own inadequacies,
partly because there are tenses
human language has yet to invent.

JOHN FOWLES

HOLY LAND

I offer six words, close neighbours in the dictionary, apt for your celebrating – holy, holly, holding, holism, home, holiday.

Holy... from many faiths comes the idea that the land, and all living things on it, are sacred. St Francis with his brother earth and sister wind; the Jain monk with his respect for all life; the aborigines with their song-lines; and the American Indians with their deep reverence...

> *Every part of this earth is sacred to my people. Every shining pine needle, every sandy shore, every mist in the dark woods, every clearing and humming insect, is holy in the memory and experience of my people. The sap which courses through the trees carries the memories of the red man, the water's murmur is the voice of my father's father.*
>
> (attributed to Chief Seattle, 1854)

This sense of sacredness in the land is felt in this country too. It expresses both divinity and the continuity of human contact over many generations. Men and women over thousands of years have tilled and changed the land, working within the constraints of nature, so that the land is rich with the inarticulate affection of folk long dead. The place vibrates with memory.

Holly... we embrace the sacred through symbols... and many of our symbols are drawn from trees. Holly, yew, mistletoe, ivy were sacred symbols for our pagan ancestors. The early church, seeking continuity, grafted new meaning on to old symbolic stock.

> *The holly bears a berry*
> *As red as any blood,*
> *And Mary bore sweet Jesus Christ*
> *To do poor sinners good.*

At Christmas, we bring this holly indoors, token of woodland, glossy with wildness, its berries plump with a bounty which we (unlike birds) cannot eat but which has meaning to us. The holly links us to the wildwood, and the wildwood to the Christ child.

Holding... we speak of a farm as a holding, a thing held, cradled, nurtured for a working lifetime, then handed on like torch from runner to runner. This is not a concept of ownership or dominion, for men to do as they please to squander or despoil. Rather is it a concept of stewardship, of care, of betterment through a lifetime so that we hand on the land to our children richer than when we came to it.

'We do not inherit the land from our parents: we borrow it from our children'.

This is the simple, long-established principle which now we cumber with the word 'sustainability'. Farmers have long understood it; and that is why so many are readily responding to the opportunities to enrich the land offered by the Devon ELMS initiative and by the Countryside Stewardship Scheme.

Holism... 'the tendency in nature to form wholes that are more than the sum of the parts by ordered grouping'
(*Concise Oxford Dictionary*).

Alas, the tendency in human society is to divide wholes into parts. Government is divided into many agencies; local government into many tiers; education into many subjects; expertise into many professions. The farmer who seeks help in managing or enhancing his land may have to seek it in bits, from many different bodies.

But such systems do violence to nature. a farm is a unit of land, a home, a business: change in one part affects another. Our systems should be flexed to fit such unities. It is good that the Devon ELMS scheme seeks to address landscape, wildlife, recreation, rural economy and the quality of rural life, all in one scheme.

Home... the warm word, describing one's own place.

Our ancestors, once settled, took rootedness for granted, keeping what Thomas Gray described as 'the noiseless tenor of their way'. In our more volatile, restless world, people move frequently: continuity, and kinship links, are often lost. Moreover, fast news from round the globe disturbs our calm: standardised culture overlaps and obscures the specialness of each place.

People are now reacting against this. They seek again a decentralised life, with roots in a locality. They wish to see a place as home, and they care about its quality as well as its cost. From the Greek word 'oikos' (house, or home) come two key concepts – ecology and economy – which reflect this combination of quality and cost. We must learn to reconcile, and to fuse, the two concepts.

Holiday... this word sprang from the Biblical injunction to rest on the seventh day... the holy day, the day of festivity or recreation. For many, it was a day outdoors, enjoying nature. Wordsworth describes how, as a five-year-old child, he

> *... Made one long bathing of a summer's day;*
> *Basked in the sun, and plunged and basked again*
> *Alternate, all a summer's day or scoured*
> *The sandy fields, leaping through flowery groves*
> *of yellow ragwort...*

The same delight in sun and water brings families in their tens of thousands out into the countryside at weekends and holidays. Visits to the countryside are precious elements in the quality of life of millions, whether they live in town or country. They may no longer care for Biblical injunctions: Sundays are no longer the only days of rest: but human instinct draws them out to the peace and quiet, the live green countryside, where the whole and the holy dwell.

MICHAEL DOWER

This old land turns like a waggon wheel,
a Sunday peace,
serene with memory, and the prospect of lambs.

LEONARD CLARK

BULLATON FARMSTEAD

Bullaton Farmstead is the subject of an ELMS-supported project being undertaken as part of a management agreement between the Dartmoor National Park Authority (DNPA) and the owners, Jonathan and Caroline Seward. The farm, 60 hectares of rolling Devon pasture, has been in the Seward family for three generations. At the heart of the land is the farmstead – a late medieval farmhouse surrounded by agricultural buildings of eighteenth and nineteenth century date, and the remains of old orchards. It has been described as 'one of the best historic farmsteads on Dartmoor.' The buildings are attractive and interesting in their own right, as good examples of traditional architecture, but one particular magic they offer is that they evoke an age of farming now past, an age before the discovery of the internal combustion engine, when farms had to be much more self-sufficient and less focused in what they produced.

These buildings and structures tell us of the way Bullaton was farmed a hundred – and more – years ago. The threshing barn and granary show us that cereals were being grown and the root store suggests fields of turnips and potatoes where now there is only grass. The grain destined for the granary was beaten from the straw by a machine worked by a horse walking endlessly in a circle in the enginehouse at the back of the barn. The rick-stands – possibly a unique feature in Devon – speak of haymeadows, the linhay of cattle spending the winter months in the shelter of the farmyard. Pigs lived in very superior accommodation behind the farmhouse, each sty with its own fully-fitted granite trough. The pigswill was prepared in the washhouse close by. At one end of the pigsties is a two-seater earth closet, or latrine, a visit to which necessitated a tramp across the garden from the house. There are sheds for carts and traps, stables for horses and a tiny building for storing ash from the family fire for use as a fertiliser on the kitchen garden. Thus is history written in stone and wood as well as books. For the owners, the farm buildings are where Great Uncle Frank spent his working life, and others before him, and they provide an attractive and protective setting for the farmhouse. But farming methods have changed and the barns can no longer serve as they once did. When Jonathan and Caroline took the farm over, the buildings were in a sad state of decay and on the point of falling down. The Seward's concern that this should not be allowed to happen was the trigger which set this project in motion.

The DNPA's management agreements are usually concerned with the protection and conservation of an area of high landscape, nature conservation or archaeological value rather than buildings. But the traditional buildings of the farmstead are an integral part of the landscape and the hub from which the wider landscape was shaped and worked. The historic relationship between the farmed land and the farmstead is symbiotic, one of mutual dependence. Without the one, there would not be the other.

The refurbishment of the dilapidated buildings has represented a departure from what is normally understood by 'conservation'. But for us, it has offered an irresistible combination of opportunities. The salvage of a landscape feature and of one of the finest collections and rare survivals of vernacular farm buildings in the county. A demonstration of good repair and a means of recalling the past to the present. A project of partnership, the DNPA, ELMS and not least, of course, the owners.

DEBBIE GRIFFITHS

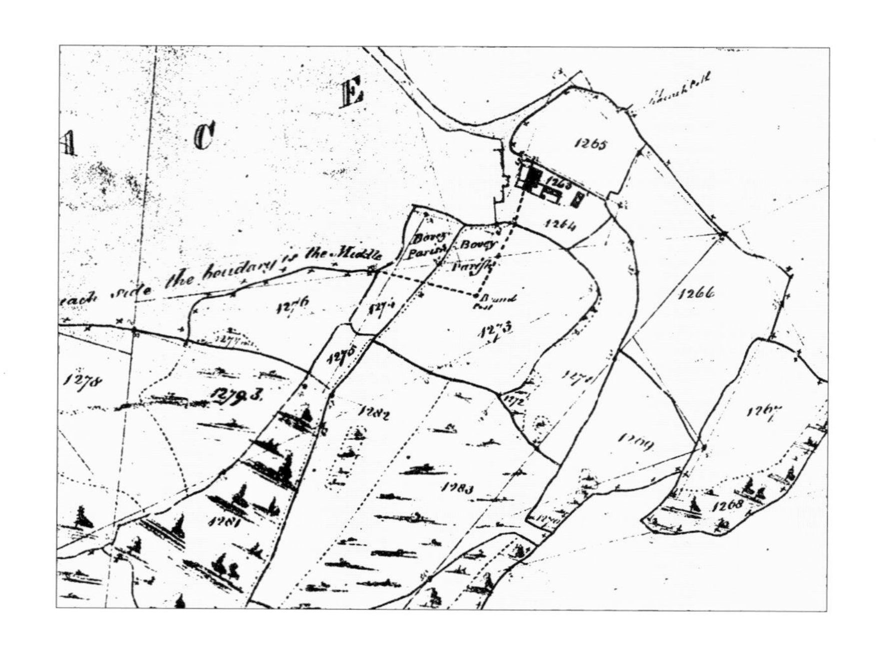
C
E
1265
1264
Bovey Parish
Bovey Parish
each side the boundary to the Middle
1276
1273
1266
1282
1283
1281
1268

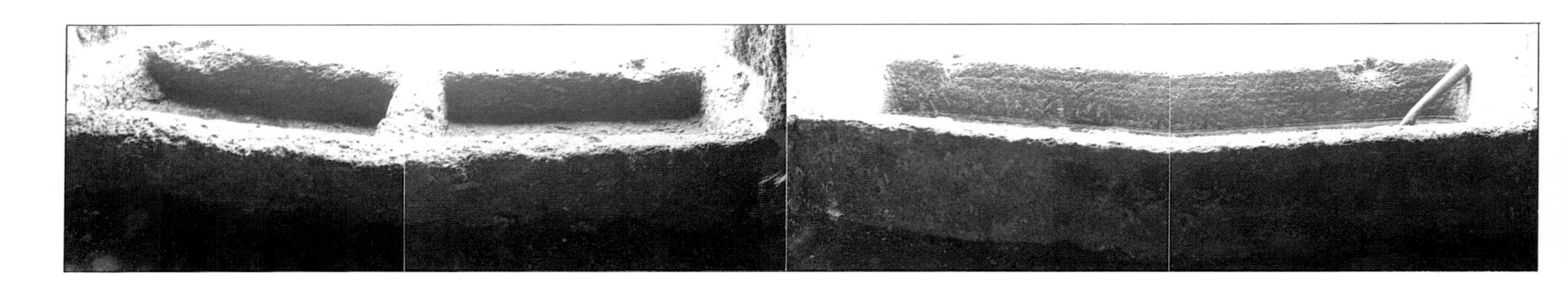

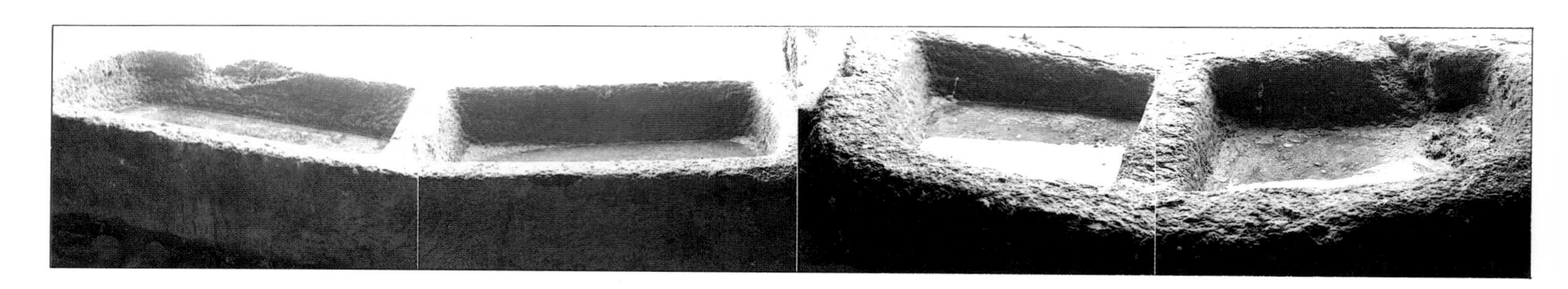

BRADFORD BARTON

When we decided to buy Bradford Barton in the spring of 1991, it wasn't just the well-preserved traditional stone farmbuildings or the untouched Devon longhouse with the possibly hitherto hidden inglenook fireplace that attracted us, but also the dilapidated orchard which was crying out for somebody to take pity. There were many fallen, dead old trees, mountains of brambles, thistles and stinging nettles higher than eight feet. My husband absolutely loves trees and has always planted trees in all our former gardens, but this was a real challenge, 5.5 acres of orchard with many bare areas. With support from ELMS, 150 cider apple trees were ordered!

Once the orchard was fenced, we could have sheep grazing, which would keep the grass down. It was wonderful to see the shape of the orchard emerge, first you could not see further than twenty feet and your view was obstructed. Now you can see a gently sloping meadow with the most wonderfully curved and shaped trees. Some are over a hundred years old and some just planted. The orchard always reminds me of life itself. Old trees, bent over and crooked but still bearing fruit and holding on to life, then some splendid specimens, laden with apples in the autumn and in the middle of their lifespan, then the young, newly planted trees, bearing fruit the first time, giving hardly any shade but growing quietly and unobserved.

I love the atmosphere in our orchard. It might be a windy day coming from the north or west but the moment you shut the gate behind you, the wind seems to drop and the air becomes calm. You are sheltered within whispering living trees.

The orchard most wonderfully represents the changing seasons. The best time is May with spectacular blossoms. The air is filled with the humming sound of hundreds of birds, bees and insects. In the heat of the summer the sheep find shade under the trees and are able to sleep and relax. In October and November the trees are laden and the ground beneath is covered with apples of all shapes and sizes. We even have two trees, where the apples are plum-shaped and the flesh is red all through like a blood orange. That of course gives our cider the wonderful rich colour. I love picking apples and observing my neatly stacked sacks full of apples, pondering how many presses of cider we will have. I cannot bear to leave any but seem to have a compulsion to gather them all. Then winter comes and to walk in the orchard on a beautiful frosty morning is an experience. The frost has settled on all the old branches that are covered with lichen and has created the most bizarre shapes. The frozen grass crunches under your feet and you know it has all been worthwhile.

RENATE HUCKLE

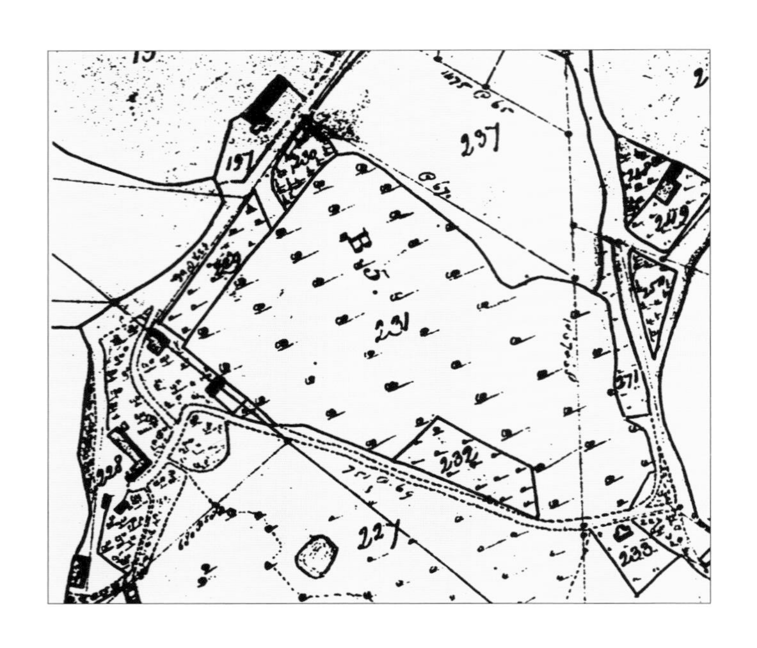

"Who planted this old apple-tree?"
The children of that distant day
Thus to some aged man shall say;

And gazing on its mossy stem,
The gray- haired man shall answer them:
"A poet of the land was he,

'Tis said he made some quaint old rhymes
On planting the apple-tree."

William Cullen Bryant (1794-1878)

WASSAILING

The *Oxford English Dictionary* defines the noun 'wassail' as a festive occasion or drinking bout and also as the kind of liquor drunk on such occasions, while the verb 'wassail' means to make merry.

The Christmas drink was the wassail, whose name is still preserved in old carols. It consisted of ale, roast apples, eggs, sugar, nutmegs, cloves and ginger served in an apple-wood bowl and drunk hot. Wassailers would carry the bowl from door to door and people would fill it with ale or cider to make sure of a good apple harvest – a relic of ancient tree worship.

By the end of the nineteenth century carol-singing had generally become an excuse for begging. Children went from door to door, banged on the knocker, and asked for what might be called 'hush money'. Carol singing had merged with the ancient custom of wassailing. In the Middle ages, wassailers (from the Anglo-Saxon word *washael* meaning 'good health') carried round a bowl of ale with ribbons on it during the last week of Advent to share with every household. As time went on, an empty bowl was used instead and the unfortunate neighbours were expected to give rather than receive.

One of the better known wassail songs has the verse:

Here we come a-wassailing
Among the leaves so green
Here we come a-wandering
So fair to be seen.

Robert Herrick, the poet who spent many years at Dean Prior in Devon may well have been referring to local customs when he wrote:

I sing of brooks, of blossoms, birds and bowers:
Of April, May, of June and July flowers
I sing of May poles, Hock-carts, wassails, wakes,
Of bride-grooms, brides and their bridal cakes.

In the Westcountry and in some other parts of the country there is an old custom of wassailing cider apple trees to encourage a good crop in the coming year. The ceremony by tradition takes place after the start of the New Year and is determined by the old calendar.

There are several wassail songs. One goes like this:

Here's to thee, old apple tree
Whence thou may'st bud, and whence thou may'st blow!
And whence thou must bear apples enow
Hats full! Caps full!
Bushel-bushel-sacks full
And in my pockets full, too. Hurrah!

Details of cider wassailing vary but often involve putting toast soaked in mulled cider into the branches of the apple trees and firing shot-guns at them, presumably to drive away evil spirits.

TIM WILLIAMS

• Apple tree prosper, bud, bloom and bear, That we may have plenty of cider next year. And where there's a barrel, we hope that there are ten, That we may have cider when we come again. •
A-wassail, a-wassail! The Moon, she shines down: The apples are ripe and the nuts they are brown. Whence thou mayest bud, dear old apple tree, And whence thou mayest bear, we sing unto thee.

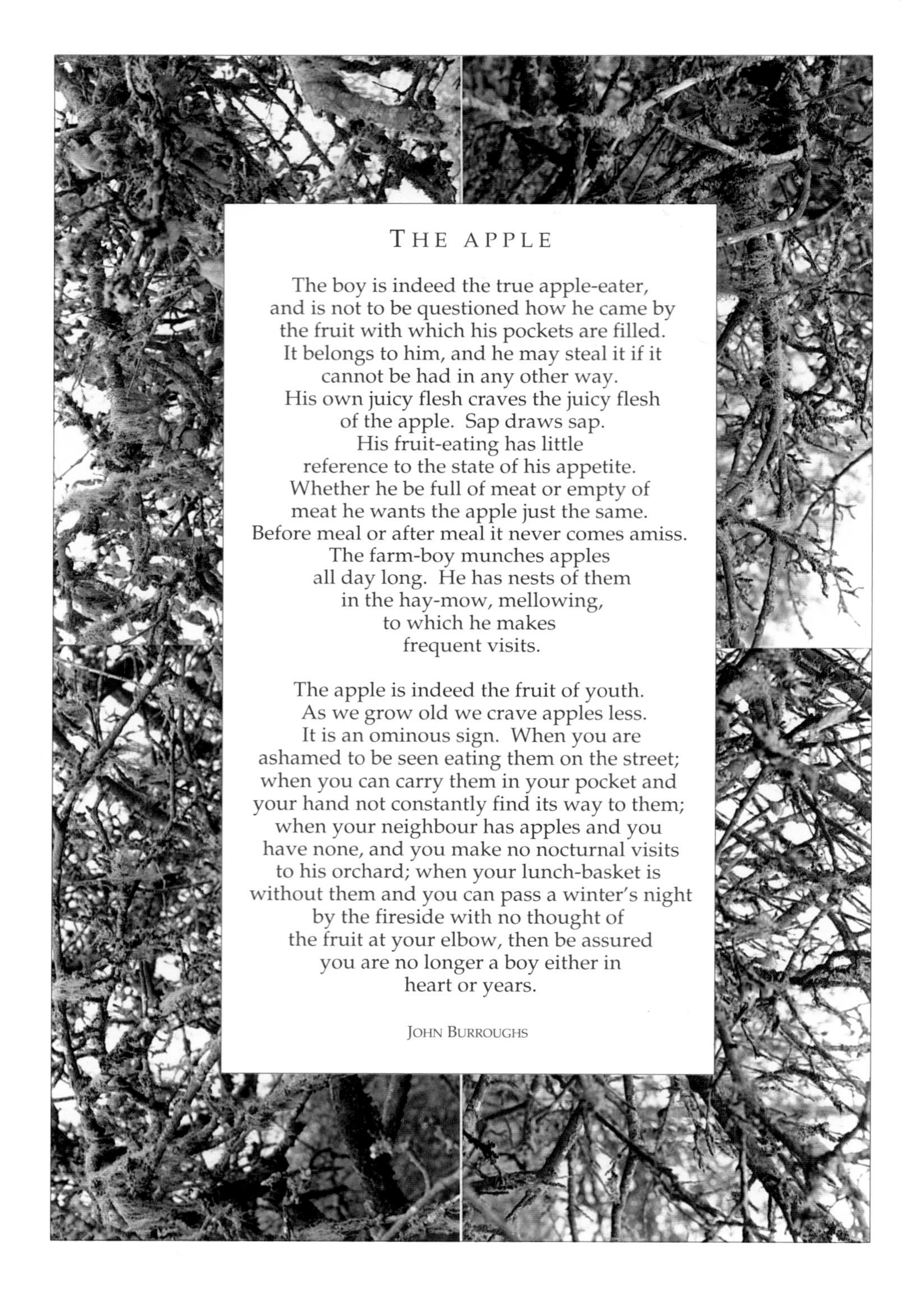

THE APPLE

The boy is indeed the true apple-eater,
and is not to be questioned how he came by
the fruit with which his pockets are filled.
It belongs to him, and he may steal it if it
cannot be had in any other way.
His own juicy flesh craves the juicy flesh
of the apple. Sap draws sap.
His fruit-eating has little
reference to the state of his appetite.
Whether he be full of meat or empty of
meat he wants the apple just the same.
Before meal or after meal it never comes amiss.
The farm-boy munches apples
all day long. He has nests of them
in the hay-mow, mellowing,
to which he makes
frequent visits.

The apple is indeed the fruit of youth.
As we grow old we crave apples less.
It is an ominous sign. When you are
ashamed to be seen eating them on the street;
when you can carry them in your pocket and
your hand not constantly find its way to them;
when your neighbour has apples and you
have none, and you make no nocturnal visits
to his orchard; when your lunch-basket is
without them and you can pass a winter's night
by the fireside with no thought of
the fruit at your elbow, then be assured
you are no longer a boy either in
heart or years.

JOHN BURROUGHS

MAKING CIDER

A holiday from field and dung,
From plough and harrow, scythe and spade,
To dabble in another trade,
To crush the pippins in the slats,
And see that in the little vats
An extra pint was wrung;
While round about the worthies stood,
Profuse in comment, praise or blame,
Content the press should be of wood,
Advising rum, decrying wheat,
And black strong sugar makes it sweet,
But still resolved, with maundering tongue,
That cider could not be the same
As once when they were young;
But still the young contemptuous men
Laughed kindly at their old conceit,
And strained upon the crank again.

VITA SACKVILLE-WEST

SHUTE HILL

If you stand and look south from the top of Shute Hill, you will have a panoramic view of the East Devon coastline, the sea and on clear days Torbay and Dartmoor. Four years ago in 1989 you would have seen a thicket of pine and cedar trees about twenty years old. Hidden amongst the rhododendron and brambles was the remains of an Armada Beacon which was known to the locals as the site was occasionally used by people walking their dogs.

On 25 January 1990, the severe gales devastated Shute Hill woodlands. Since that time it has been a process of rebuilding and planning again for the future. Despite the tragedy of the gales and the damage that they caused some good will come as a result.

As managers of these woodlands, we have been involved at Shute for nearly fifteen years. The woodlands have been managed principally for the production of commercial timber and this, inevitably, means the planting of a majority of conifers with wide rides made accessible to local people.

We have always been aware, since taking on the management of the woodlands, that it would have been necessary to plan for the felling of these mature trees. A plan had been produced for the 're-structuring' of the woodlands following commercial felling and it was fairly simple to put this plan into effect following the 1990 gales.

Having suddenly found ourselves with some magnificent views from the top of the hill and the ancient monument of local interest, we were approached by East Devon District Council to see whether we could facilitate some form of public access so that people could enjoy the site in an informal way but also in a controlled way. Fortunately, the landowners saw the benefits that this scheme would bring to the site, especially at time of great change. It is one thing not to oppose people walking in the woodland situation, but to actively invite people into the site is a big commitment on the owners' part and their managers, especially regarding safety and maintenance.

The ELMS scheme has allowed us to create car parking facilities, waymarking of walks, making safe the site and, importantly, we are able to restore the Beacon and provide information for visitors. The woodland is also included in the Forestry Trust's handbook of woodlands to visit and is called a 'Study Wood'. We also hope that it will become a Forestry Authority 'Centre of Excellence', an example of what can be achieved in promoting public access to private woodlands.

ALASTAIR SANDELS MSc MICFor
AREA FORESTER
FOUNTAIN FORESTRY LTD

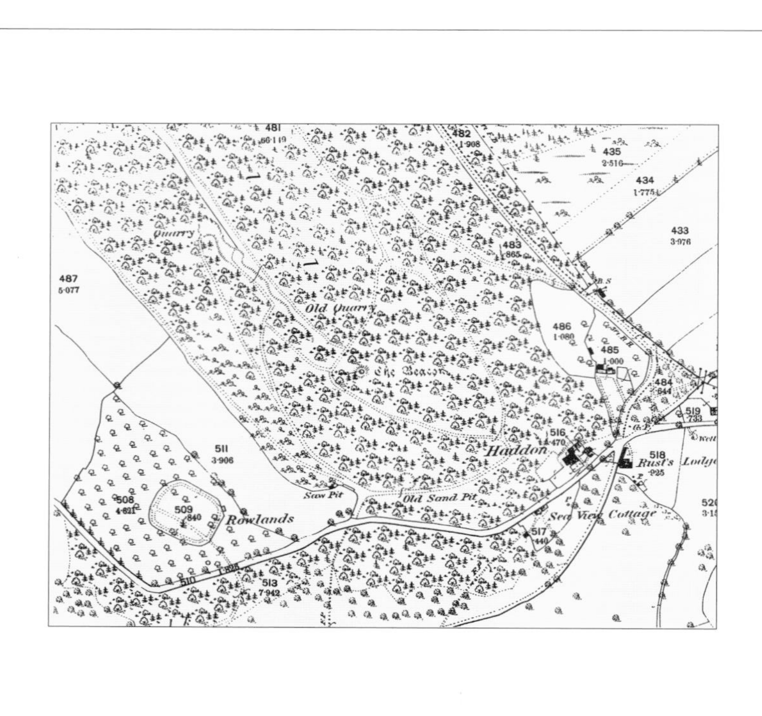
481
66·119
482
1·908
435
2·516
434
1·775
433
3·976
Quarry
483
865
487
5·077
Old Quarry
486
1·080
485
1·000
The Beacon
484
·644
519
·733
511
3·906
516
·470
Haddon
518
Rust's
·925
Saw Pit
Old Sand Pit
508
4·621
509
·840
Rowlands
Sea View Cottage
517
·440
510
1·828
513
7·942

DRAGONFLIES OVER SHUTE HILL

If dragonflies made war they would carry cameras and head for Shute Hill in Devon.

They would then return to their base at the foot of the hill on the banks of the River Axe.

Soon they would be peering over a patchwork quilt of aerial photographs.

Each photograph would slightly overlap its neighbours but the overall picture would be an accurate record of a landscape.

The dragonflies would then send in a bomber force of newly hatched nymphs. Warfare is for real and the dragonfly nymph is really a goggle-eyed torpedo with legs.

Shute Hill has seen a lot of warfare.

Men were chipping its stones long before Jesus was nailed to the cross.

The Romans built a road over the hill during their relentless pursuit of empire building.

Today the road is no more than an arrow of ink on the Ordnance Survey map.

Its foundation of flint has been recycled, propping up the Church and cottages of the nearby Saxon village of Kilmington.

Other boulders were later used to build a beacon on the hill.

The network of bonfires that saved a nation is not unlike the pattern on the wing of the dragonfly.

The sweet-chestnut trees that thrive on Shute hill are reminders – if not direct descendants – of the fruits of Celtic slave labour.

What has probably gone forever is a species of lobelia, once common in the fields around Shute and Kilmington. It grew nowhere else in the world.

"...picture the wolf-packs collecting in the dense sombre woods which then clothed the hill-sides far and near! Easy to fancy the kite and the raven in the grey morning sky, swooping ominously over the marsh plain and startling the red deer which slakes its thirst in the as yet unbloodstained stream!"

This quotation is from the *Book of the Axe* written by George Philip Rigney Pulman and first published in 1871.

Mr Pulman throws up one image after another of one of the bloodiest battles ever fought on English soil.

Pulman died before the onset of the First World War.

The soldiers which followed him are honoured in the churchyards that abut his sacred river.

The new generation exploring Shute Hill and the Axe will enjoy the Brimstone and the Red Admiral.

But it should know that these butterflies and their caterpillars are vegetarians.

They evolved long after the dragonfly, whose ancestry goes back to the carboniferous period, some three hundred million years ago.

In those days dragonflies sported a two foot wing span.

Like all insects, dragonflies are ruled by instinct and warfare is perhaps instinctive in mankind.

The Emperor Dragonfly that occasionally hunts over Shute has a pair of compound eyes.

Each eye looks like honeycombe when viewed under a microscope, not unlike the mosaic of hedgerows that we used to know.

Dr Colin Dawes

THE ENVIRONMENT AND THE HUMAN SPIRIT

It is perhaps that scientific rationalism for all its wondrous achievements has practised upon us a great deception – suggesting to us that we are overlords of all we survey, 'taming' nature, placing the environment at our service, that – in short – collectively we have become God on Earth? Let me go a little further with the exploration, and invoke a little help from those who can express such ideas better ever than I.

It dances today my heart, like a peacock it dances it dances.
It sports a mosaic of passions like a peacock's tail,
It soars to the sky with delight, it quests, O wildly,
It dances today, my heart, like a peacock it dances.

Storm-clouds roll through the sky, vaunting their thunder,
their thunder.
Rice-plants bend and sway as the water rushes,
Frogs croak, doves huddle and tremble in their nests, O proudly,
Storm-clouds roll through the sky vaunting their thunder...

That fragment is from a poem called *New Rain* by Rabindranath Tagore. No delusion in his vision that man is in control, taming nature. On the contrary the surge of joy that he describes springs from the knowledge that man is at one with the elements, dependent on them – as part of the natural world.

And yet so many of us in this half of the twentieth century rarely if ever hear the moan of the wind in the trees, the hissing of rain on grass, the cry of birds above fields, the sound of silence in the wind. Instead we are cocooned behind the shutters of urban life, cocooned and marooned. And therefore it takes the sensitivity of the great imaginative intellects to transport us back to ourselves, to re-discover ourselves in nature.

Thus Herman Hesse:

Sometimes when a bird cries out
or the wind sweeps through a tree
or a dog howls in a far-off farm
I hold still and listen a long time.

My world turns and goes back to the place
where, a thousand forgotten years ago,
the bird and blowing wind
were like me, and were my brothers.

My soul turns into a tree,
and an animal, and a cloud bank.
Then changed and odd it comes home
and asks me questions. What should I reply?

The identity of man with nature is not of course supposed to define a literal conjunction. It is rather a spiritual expression of a widely known but underestimated and often forgotten fact. Mankind depends on sun, on air, and on water. So does every living creature, every living plant. We partake – all of us – of the same substances for our survival. And the great connector between those elements and all living things is the earth.

Thomas Wendell Berry, the American poet and farmer, wrote an essay called simply 'The Use of Energy'. This is a brilliantly expressed critique of a still prevailing belief that sources of energy are limitless, and may therefore be consumed with impunity. The only sense in which it is precisely appropriate to speak of limitless energy is in respect of what Berry calls 'biological energy'. What he writes has impeccable scientific credentials but is expressed in terms which reveal a profound spiritual insight, rich in paradox:

> *The soil is the healer and restorer and resurrector, by which disease passes into health, age into youth, death into life. Without proper care for it we can have no community, because without proper care for it we can have no life.*
>
> *It is alive itself. It is a grave, too, of course. Or a healthy soil is. It is full of dead animals and plants, bodies that have passed through other bodies... The only way into the soil is through other bodies. But no matter how finely the dead are broken down, or how many times they are eaten, they yet give into other life. If a healthy soil is full of death it is also full of life: worms, fungi, micro-organisms of all kinds, for which, as for us humans, the dead bodies of the once living are a feast. Eventually this dead matter becomes soluble, available as food for plants, and life begins to rise up again, out of the soil into the light. Given only the health of the soil, nothing that dies is dead for very long... It is impossible to contemplate the life of the soil for very long without seeing it as analogous to the life of the spirit.*

In the beauty and simplicity of that prose there is revealed a profound and ancient truth, of which organic farmers – until recently mocked as brown-sandalled eccentrics – have been at pains to persuade us for many years.

The American poet Walt Whitman, expressing the same truth, takes the next step, writing:

> *We are nature, long have we been absent, but now we return,*
> *we become plants, trunks, foliage, roots, bark,*
> *we are bedded in the ground, we are rocks,*
> *we are oaks, we grow in the openings side by side...*

And among a host of others likewise, the Navajo chant:

> *The mountains I become a part of it.*
> *The herbs, the fir tree I become a part of it.*
> *The morning mists, the clouds, the gathering waters,*
> *I become a part of it.*
> *The wilderness, the dew-drops, the pollen,*
> *I became part of it.*

And once more, the fourteenth-century Abbess (and incidentally first female composer!) Hildegarde of Bingen, writing so many centuries ago:

> *I am the breeze that nurtures all things green.*
> *I encourage blossoms to flourish with ripening fruits.*
> *I am led by the spirit to feed the purest streams.*
> *I am the rain coming from the dew*
> *that causes the grasses to laugh with the joy of life.*
> *I am the yearning for good.*

These poems are a devout expression of what – I suppose – might rather prosaically be called our ecological identity, our oneness, our inextricable oneness, with the natural world and the natural order. But a oneness from which we have become separated.

If we are stricken by the false belief that there is no necessary connection between ourselves and the natural world, if we are to recover ourselves, our inner selves, our wholeness as individuals, then perhaps we should attend rather more closely to this relationship with the natural world, our understanding of it: its cycles and its harmonies.

I hesitate to plunge into James Lovelock's Gaia hypothesis or the General Systems Theory – not least because I am ill-equipped to do so. But their overlapping ideas for me at least enormously illuminate in biological terms what the poets said in the language of the imagination and the senses.

Crudely summarised, General Systems Theory (the first exposition of which is credited to the German biologists Weiss and Von Bertalanffy) establishes a model for examining the natural world; a model which starts from the proposition that nothing can be understood on its own, that all things form part of a system. Each system is a whole and at the same time forms part of a whole. The idea of Gaia (named after the Greek goddess, Gaia, the Earth Mother) postulates that the entire range of living matter from the smallest virus to the greatest creature forms part of a great entity that interacts with its constituent parts, and with the atmosphere, the sea, and the soil to create the optimum conditions for survival on our planet. Touch one and every other is affected. Throw a stone in the water and you know not where the wave stops.

In medicine the practice of complementary therapies is closely linked to these biological perceptions. As Patrick Pietroni, an outstanding theorist and practitioner has pointed out, 'green' medicine with its focus on healing is closely allied to an appreciation of the natural order of things. Alternative medicine or complementary medicine insists that the whole person must be treated, not one of his or her constituent parts alone. The opinion polls and the statistics tell us there is a great surge in the numbers of those turning to such therapies because they offer a remedy that orthodox treatments cannot provide.

The hospice movement which used to be regarded at best as quirky if not quacklike is now established as the living essence of this holistic approach, placing the human spirit at the heart of the matter.

My point in referring to these things – as a novitiate – is to reach towards an interim conclusion. My feeling is – and it is not more than this – that we may be at a point of re-awakening or of re-discovery.

To re-capture this spirit involves a re-discovery of our place in the natural world, our re-integration into that world. How is this to be achieved?

It is an obvious nonsense to presume that we can live only for today because tomorrow will care for itself. To ignore this, as all recognise, would be a cruel practical joke visited on generations as yet unborn.

And YES: we do now fear for the rain-forests; we do care about lost species; we worry about whales; holes in the ozone layer alarm us; the greenhouse effect is a household concept; pollution of the oceans and the beaches offends us. All of this is greatly for the good, a huge advance in the space of but a few years.

But that concern and that care remains terribly susceptible to short-term vagaries and the instant political fix. It is a political commonplace that in the recession environmental concern has taken a back seat, and that it will return to the forefront of the public mind only with the recovery. The inference is obvious:

in our polity – except where we are strapped in by law – concern for the environment is still at the margins, an afterthought, a luxury. And the politicians adjust their priorities accordingly.

If we are to advance from this casual opportunism, it must surely be when a concern for the environment is more naturally integrated into our habit of thought and belief. If, as I've suggested, the human spirit needs to re-discover the natural world, it is also true that the protection of the natural world requires a commitment from the human spirit.

It follows – naturally if not logically – that we may better serve the needs of the Self and the needs of the Environment if we can establish a happier balance, a closer harmony, between our material aspirations and our metaphysical yearnings.

I do not think that such a project is easy to accomplish but I am not a pessimist. I am confident that I am not stumbling towards these notions alone. There may not be a collective unconscious, but there is, I sense, a groundswell of thought, feeling and intuition that tells me I am not entirely barking – either up the wrong tree or mad! Or that if I am then many others are as well.

As I was hoping I was right about that I stumbled on an article in *Farmers Weekly*, a specialist journal which prides itself on having its feet planted on *terra firma*. It is not given to flights of fancy. And there is an article asserting precisely this point: that the agricultural community would have to recover its spiritual identity – or 'spiritualism' as the writer put it. He argued that the times demanded this both for the sake of the physical environment and for the purpose of giving effective expression to a growing public mood.

Then, and also by chance, I came across an essay by the novelist John Fowles and rejoiced to find this:

> *Keats' attitude towards the nightingale has very arguably more scientific validity than that of the worthy gentlemen who pursued the bird with brass dividers and rulers. All the hard taxonomic facts in the world don't add up to the reality of the nightingale; and if a visitor from Outer Space wanted to know that reality, he would do much better with the* Ode *than the* Handbook of British Birds...

He allows that this may sound dangerously like the Romantic Movement's Theory of Nature but declares: 'I think we, in our present, vilely polluted world, had better think twice before we sneer the Romantic Theory into oblivion.' And he reminds us that the Romantics were part of the reaction to 'a cerebral and artificial age which would have raped nature quite as abominably as ourselves if it had had the technology and population at hand.'

For John Fowles the Romantic Theory 'reasserted the identity of man and nature, the dangers of splitting that identity'. And in this unabashed statement of his love for the natural world, he surely speaks for the aching human soul that cannot find the words: 'It reconciles me with the imperfections of my own condition, of our whole human condition, of the all that is. My freedom depends totally on its freedom. Without my freedom, I should not want to live.'

So what can we do? Or perhaps – what is to be done? Campaigning, of course, for policies that are wise and sensitive and which speak to our common humanity. To campaign – as the Council for the Preservation of Rural England campaigns, and all manner of other similarly minded organisations and individuals – mustering the technical and scientific data and then deploying the evidence in careful and reasoned argument. That of course is crucial.

But also – sometimes – we should reflect on the questions which I have tentatively addressed, seeking to approach the question 'why?' And then sometimes we might allow ourselves the awakening suspicion that, in doing so, we are reflecting that great – universal – human need which the writers, poets and thinkers to whom I have referred so wonderfully express. And that means to the inner self as well as the outer world.

Schumacher wrote: 'Everywhere people ask "What can I actually do?"'. And he went on:

> *The answer is as simple as it is disconcerting: we can, each of us, work to put our inner house in order. The guidance for this work cannot be found in science or technology, the value of which depends entirely on the ends they serve; but it can still be found in the traditional wisdom of mankind.*

In this sense there is no advance, there is no retreat. It is there to be re-discovered. And it is there to explain ourselves to ourselves. When our brains are worried to ribbons by the complexity of the issues with which environmentalists grapple, by the endless host of campaigns to stop this motorway, or to protect those fields or that wood, to advance this planning strategy or to resist that, to sustain a vital cause over weeks, months and years, without flagging, in good humour, and with commonsense as well as zeal, then I think you can find nurture in that 'wisdom of mankind' that gives meaning to the action, beyond the local and particular, the here and now. That in its very permanence gives hope and inspiration.

Here to end is but one example from the American Indian Chief, Seattle, that reminds us of a great truth that embraces the Self and the natural world, and our responsibilities to both. Such understanding must surely be at the heart of the environmental project, not EVER at its periphery:

> *Teach your children*
> *what we have taught our children –*
> *that the Earth is our Mother.*
> *Whatever befalls the Earth*
> *befalls the sons and daughters of the Earth.*
> *If men spit upon the ground,*
> *they spit upon themselves.*
>
> *This we know*
> *the Earth does not belong to us,*
> *we belong to the Earth.*
>
> *This we know*
> *all things are connected*
> *like the blood which unites one family*
> *all things are connected.*
>
> *Whatever befalls the Earth*
> *befalls the sons and daughters of the Earth.*
> *We did not weave the web of life,*
> *we are merely a strand in it.*
>
> *Whatever we do to the web,*
> *we do to ourselves.*

(Extracted from a paper delivered as one of the Schumacher Lectures, 1993.)

JONATHAN DIMBLEBY
30th September 1993

HIGHER CADHAM

Higher Cadham Farm is a 139-acre mixed farm. At present we have 440 ewes, 12 suckler cows, plus followers. It is a family farm on which my wife runs a successful bed and breakfast business from Easter to November (after lambing). The permissive path which we provided through the farmyard, across the meadow and over the bridge to the public footpath to Exbourne (part of the Tarka Trail) is now very popular with locals doing a short circular walk around Jacobstowe as well as dedicated walkers who follow the complete Tarka Trail. Without an ELMS grant to assist with the bridge, this route would not have been possible as the River Okement separates the farm into two blocks.

We have now gone into The Countryside Stewardship Scheme giving the public more access. We also have a hardcore footpath from the farmyard to the river so that the less mobile may also enjoy the countryside, the bridge and the soothing river, and perhaps see one of our kingfishers, or if very lucky an otter.

There is a lot more wildlife, birds and dragonflies on the farm pond where you can feed the ducks and watch them feeding off the bottom.

As I said Higher Cadham is a family farm. My grandfather came here in 1910. My father was born here and took over on his marriage in 1938. I was born here and took over from my father when I married in January 1976. We have two daughters, Julie 16 and Alison 11. What the future holds for the next generation is anyone's guess.

JOHN KING

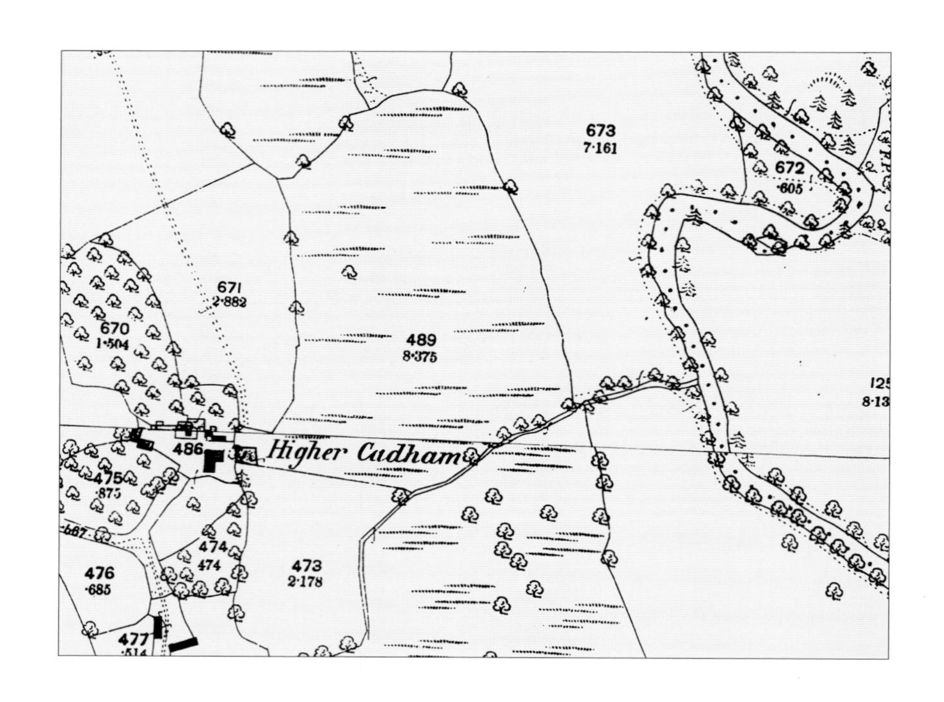
673
7·161
672
·605
671
2·882
670
1·504
489
8·375
125
8·13
486
Higher Cadham
475
·875
667
474
474
476
·685
473
2·178
477

'The river is stuffed with otters', is a remark made at a conservation meeting which I shall never forget. Such erroneous and misleading comments are the worst kind, even if well meant, for they can lead to complacency. Somewhere in amongst it all lies the truth and the truth is otters are holding their own in some areas but are still an endangered species as far as Britain as a whole is concerned.

The reason for this is easy to understand and difficult to rectify and it applies to almost all species of flora and fauna which cannot adapt – and perhaps should not have to adapt – to the ever increasing pressures of human activity on the countryside. Perhaps the otter, of all creatures, is emerging as the one which stands as a 'marker' to the way things are going not just for wildlife but also for humans.

It would be good to think our love for otters and other wild creatures, and plants too, helps us understand them and thus ourselves.

A conservationist has to be an optimist. Optimism will see us through. People like Philip Wayre of the 'Otter Trust' and Vincent Weir of the 'Vincent Wildlife Trust' cared about otters and had the wherewithal to do something about it. Today we all know about breeding and release programmes and about 'Otter Havens'. Both have been successful in their own way and have taught us much about otters and their needs.

Optimism is the Mother of Vision. The sort of vision that sees ahead, sees through obstacles to a final, beautiful truth and result. It is the bit in the middle, the getting rid of obstacles be they pollution, apathy, red-tape or whatever, that is the hardest.

That's where 'Everyman' comes in. We almost need a 'Project Everyman'. The otters need such a project, as do dippers, kingfishers, primroses, oak trees, the lot.

We may feel we have it. There's the RSPB, the County Naturalist Trusts, World Fund for Wildlife, etc. etc. etc! But it is not enough. All are doing their bit and as they grow they themselves cost more to survive! We do not need our conservation organisations as 'endangered species'.

So let US learn from friend otter. My own observations on otters in the West Country and in Scotland over many years show they are creatures who live by their needs, as do most creatures and plants. The question is can we do the same? Have we as individuals got the courage to live by our needs despite the various pressures to see that we don't?

What has this got to do with otters, did someone say? Well, it has got everything to do with otters, for if we do not practice conservation and a wise use of resources to the full there may well not be any otters.

Elms were my favourite trees. I grew up with elm trees in every hedgerow across North Devonshire where I was born. Millions of them there were. Sadly I cannot take my youngsters for a walk and point them out!

If we are very lucky and keep trying for a few summer's evenings I can eventually show them an otter, or perhaps their footprints.

It is the otter itself and its plight as an endangered species, and a bit of the Henry Williamson magic, that has brought us all together to share active concern for the countryside. The projects chosen within this book shows but a tiny fraction of what is really happening out there in Devon, in the West Country and in Britain, for nature conservation, and maybe we will have hedgerows of elms, and rivers 'stuffed with otters' someday.

TREVOR BEER

UNTITLED
(for Beverly)

On the table
under the lamp
are three pebbles
I brought from Dieppe

Often when I eat
drink coffee or talk
they interrupt
the trains of my thought

One is green coloured
long and thick
and it lunges on the cloth
like a fish

The second is brown
and open with a tongue
when I first saw it
I thought of a muzzle

The third is oval
dark grey in net of white
regular and haphazard
it reminds me of nothing

When the stones interrupt
I put out my hand
to touch
what I find in them

I adjust the fish
so that I can see
its eye
and the thrust of its tail

I place
my little finger
between the jaws
of the brown animal

the third pebble I pick up
hold deliberately
and place back on the table
so that

it looks to me like itself

JOHN BERGER

BLACKDOWN RINGS

The hillfort at Blackdown Rings near Loddiswell stands in thirteen acres of land and is defended by a massive earth and stone rampart with a deep outer ditch.

It was probably built soon after 400 BC when there seems to have been a marked deterioration of climate, mainly increased rainfall over Dartmoor, and the moor people tried to migrate to the lowlands. Blackdown is one of the best preserved Iron Age hillforts around Dartmoor. It lies 'just east of the great ridgeway from the moor down to the sea'.

Well over a thousand years later the Normans took advantage of the hilltop position and built a motte and bailey castle in the north-west corner. Although the particular circumstances are unknown it was probably following the conquest of Devon by William the Conqueror in 1068 and the counterattack the next year by the Ireland-based sons of Harold Godwinson who is thought to have landed at the mouth of the river Avon or in Salcombe harbour. Their arrival may account for the nine manors, south of Loddiswell, described in Domesday Book as 'being laid waste by Irishmen'.

The Blackdown Hill is recorded in 1546 as 'Blkedoune' and in 1752 William Chapple visited the site and drew a plan of 'The Rings' in his scrapbook. Woollcombe in 1827 recorded his survey of the hillfort and described the earthworks as being in 'a state of considerable perfection'. This was probably because of the thorns and bracken that had overgrown the ramparts and ditches. Furze for fuel was traditionally gathered on Blackdown but the land was enclosed during the nineteenth century. The parishioners protested and a commission was set up in 1854 to examine the right to cut furze on ten acres there.

In 1934 the Peeks of Hazelwood bought the land from Woolston Estate and in 1988 the Peek family gave the 'Rings' to the Arundell Charity which had been founded in 1591 by Sir Matthew Arundell 'for the good and be-hoof of the parishioners of Loddiswell'.

In 1991an ELMS grant was given by Devon County Council to assist in clearing the scrub and constructing a car park and picnic area. Interpretation plaques were placed at strategic points and a directional map was engraved into Dartmoor granite and erected on the highest point of the Motte from which there are excellent views over the countryside to the coast.

It was here that Iron Age people came to barter and exchange their merchandise or retreat in times of danger. A thousand years later the Norman chieftain built his timber castle for the protection of his household and to have control over the surrounding countryside. A beacon on the highest point passed on the urgent message of the danger of the approaching Spanish Armada in 1588.

Now we can roam and enjoy the views with thoughts of those who have populated the site, trodden this ground and travelled these paths in times past.

R. H. SAMPSON.

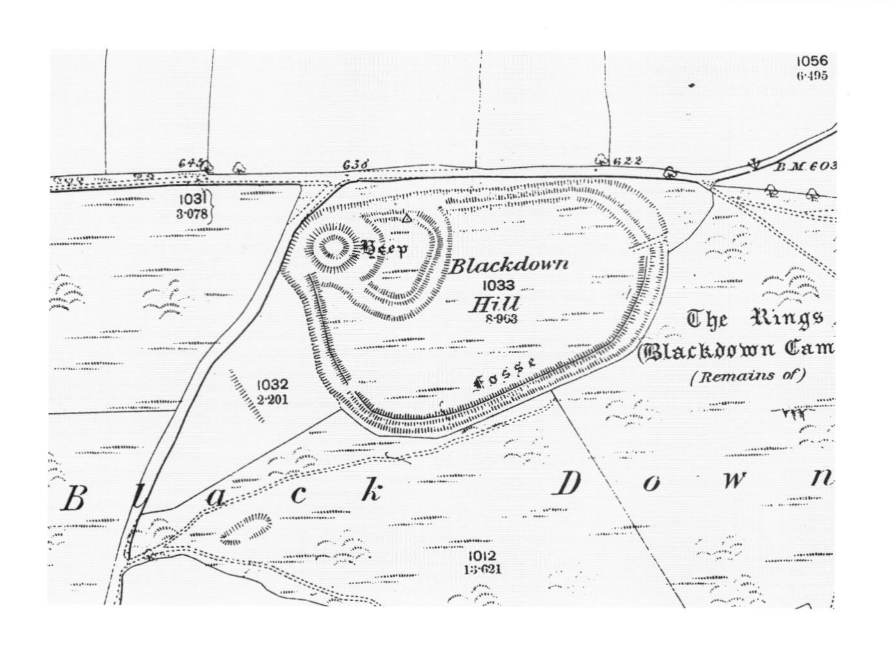
Keep
Blackdown
1033
Hill
8·963
The Rings
(Blackdown Cam
(Remains of)
Fosse
1031
3·078
1032
2·201
1012
13·621
1056
6·495
B l a c k D o w n

There were grass-grown tumuli on the hills
to which of old I used to walk, sit down at the foot of one of
them, and think. Some warrior had been interred there in the
ante-historic times. The sun of the summer morning shone on
the dome of sward, and the air came softly up from the wheat
below, the tips of the grasses swayed as it passed sighing
faintly, it ceased, and the bees hummed by to the thyme and
heathbells. I became absorbed in the glory of the day,
I felt at that moment that I was like the spirit of the man whose
body was interred in the tumulus; I could understand and feel
his existence the same as my own. He was as real to me two
thousand years after interment as those I had seen in the body.
The abstract personality of the dead seemed as existent as
thought. As my thought could slip back the twenty centuries in
a moment to the forest-days when he hurled the spear, or shot
with the bow, hunting the deer, and could return again as
swiftly to this moment, so his spirit could endure from
then till now, and the time was nothing.

RICHARD JEFFERIES

THE VALES OF DEVONIA

The Vales of Devonia!
What landscapes are seen
So fertile in beauty,
So golden and green!
There crowfoot and clover,
Allure the bee,
To gather the sweet honey
For Janie and me.
Thy hills are Devonia,
Thy meadows and streams,
They haunt me forever,
In visions and dreams;
The birds in the woodlands
Their music is rare;
Thy kine are most famous
And balmy thy air.

EDWARD CAPERN
(1819–1894)

LANDSCAPE VALUED?

A few years ago, when I was writing for an Exeter evening newspaper about the Devon environment, a man called at the office to complain bitterly about the felling of an oak tree in his village. It was, if I recall rightly, said to be endangering people who used a telephone box.

It would no doubt have been better to move the telephone kiosk than to fell the tree. But as a journalist I felt I should delve a little deeper into the matter than to accept the story on its face value alone. In the course of conversation I asked the complainant where he lived and how long he had been in the village.

He had been there eighteen months and lived in one of the new four bedroomed executive houses. I wondered how many trees had been felled, how many hedges removed and how much meadowland covered in bricks and concrete to enable him and his commuting neighbours to live in a pseudo-country environment.

The story has been repeated countless times throughout much of England, with vast swathes of countryside being swamped by road building, suburban housing estates and industrial development. A sickening and bitterly ironical lip service to what has been lost is often paid by naming roads after the very landscape that has been destroyed in this grisly march of twentieth century 'progress'.

Thus we have Meadow Drives where cows no longer chew the cud among the buttercups; BMWs stand in Linnet Crescents where once the milkmaids put down their milking stools. There are Lark Drives where no birds sing; Sylvan Drives where not even a blade of grass survives the weed-killer; Primrose Avenues from which all the wild flowers have disappeared; Orchard Views from which all that can be seen is a farm silo or two; Buttercup Lanes where the only flowers are dried ones on window sills and Woodland Closes which have a glimpse of a copse that will remain only until the bulldozers move in for the next phase of house building.

Formal, text-book gardens with obligatory cherry trees have supplanted the random riot of natural vegetation. In one place after another factory-made building material, stereo-typed architecture and mass-produced gnomes and other garden ornaments make a sickening contrast with the altogether more human mellow cottages built years ago from local materials.

Warehouses, like Martian invaders among the greensward, are surrounded with wire and concrete fence posts with a token tree or two to conform with the planning conditions. And countless old farm barns, from which the barn owls have been ousted, now sport double-glazing and carriage lamps to make their owners feel they have not left Subtopia altogether behind.

Small wonder that the countryside is said to be in danger. Many people can hardly know what it used to look as they drive down roads lined with signs about services, parking spaces and slogans shouting the odds about tourist attractions. Every year there is less genuine countryside. And every year the pressures on what is left grow more intense while the excuses for eating away at it become ever more specious.

Compared with much of the rest of the country, Devon has been incredibly lucky. Seen from the air this huge county, with the exception of its major urban areas, looks like a comfortable, sparsely populated happy green land, still with a network of hedges and dotted about with old farm buildings that blend harmoniously with the landscape.

It has many organisations which jealously guard its precious heritage. Statutory and voluntary bodies of many kinds keep a watchful eye over its built heritage and its countryside. But by far the greatest proportion of people live and work in the county's cities and towns and fewer and fewer people work on the land.

Yet it was the ancestors of many of the present urban dwellers who fashioned the landscape that so many people now wrongly regard as being a wholly natural rather than a largely man-made heritage. Unfortunately what men have made down the centuries from the time when they first started to clear the forests, can also be destroyed by men and machines – either deliberately or by neglect or by mismanagement.

But before the experts and the general public can make their views known on what should be saved and how the landscape should be conserved it is vital to know what is there. Much information on old buildings, forests, grassland, hedges, rivers and wildlife has been and is continually being collected by experts.

But rather less has been done on the assessment of landscape value. So long as it is possible for lawyers to argue at public inquiries into various controversial developments that it is impossible to put a monetary value on landscape, the easier it is for Government inspectors to ignore or play down arguments in favour of preserving a particular stretch of countryside threatened with a new section of dual carriageway or motorway, a superstore or a golf course.

Thinking of putting a monetary value on landscape is, however, the wrong way to go about it. There ought to be an acceptance that there is a moral dimension to our natural heritage and that there are natural laws which we transgress at our peril. Deprive people for long enough of the benign influence of the countryside, lock them into inner-city ghettoes and a crime wave eventually engulfs not only the city where they live but also the countryside around it.

Our political masters ought to be convinced that even though no monetary value can easily be put on landscape there should be an inbuilt recognition that there must be a presumption against destruction of countryside and wildlife habitat and that it is time the dice were loaded against motorway and office development among the green fields.

In this overcrowded little island of ours it is a limited resource which has been exploited for years past with cavalier abandon. It is common knowledge that some precious areas are so over-visited that the very things that people go there to appreciate are being seriously damaged.

The visual, aesthetic and spiritual value of a view is not limited to national parks, environmentally sensitive areas or sites of special scientific interest. Many people have a fondness for much less exalted areas. One single tree where birds sing at dusk or dawn can for some people be a bastion in their lives against the dreary world of getting and spending. Evening light over a slow moving river, even the still reflection of a misty tor in a moorland pool or a lowland pond can have a calming psychological effect. Such places are those where we have time to stand and stare.

Standing and staring with the aid of a 35mm camera may seem a thankless task to those who have taken their own photographic equipment with them to capture what they hope will be the spirit of the countryside.

But it all depends on who is using the camera. In the case of John Woodman and Roger Polley it is the vision of the men behind the lenses that counts. It is their intention to help us to see what is in front of us, but it is often not appreciated.

The stimulus from this and similar projects ought to make everybody who has a love for the countryside, or a duty to protect it, realise that somehow or another it is time that we developed not only a new way of looking at the land but reacting in a different way to it.

Woodman and Polley have achieved that task with considerable success but they would be first to admit that the totality of the countryside experience is something that is impossible to capture on photographic film alone.

It is something that is made up of a magic mixture of ingredients which include the sheer physical sensation of being out in the sun, the wind, mist, rain, frost, hail or snow. It is the sensation of treading on hard, soft, wet or springy turf. It is the satisfaction of having climbed without stopping to the top of a green hill. It is even the feel of a shirt wet with sweat on our back and feet aching from miles of walking over rough ground. It is the sound and taste of water in a fast-running stream. It is bird song. It is the dark clouds of a coming storm.

It is more than that. It is a deep folk memory of treading the green lanes and hill-top tracks where generations of men and animals have gone before. It is a heritage which we continue to destroy at our peril.

And one of its main ingredients is the smell of the country. Few things are more potent than scent. Like old tunes that haunt the memory smells can suddenly turn the clock back.

Hot tar evokes long vanished days of summer bike rides; the dry dust of harvest sheaves; the sweet smell of cider recalls hours of hard labour in the sun-soaked fields; rain on warm earth hints of new beginnings; the subtle scent of freshly-picked mushrooms sets the taste buds watering. Sawdust and sap from newly-felled trees; the fecund smell of newly ploughed earth; woodsmoke from a cottage chimney (hinting of cosy evenings by the fireside after hours in the open air) the strong stench of rotting seaweed; the unmistakable odour from a field of rotting cabbages – all have their own individual associations.

Nor is it only the earth and things that grow on it and live from it that make up the countryside. In many areas only one-third of our normal view is of the land in front of us. The rest of the visual space is filled by the sky. And just as Woodman and Polley lure us into looking at the natural world beneath our feet so too can we sometimes lie on our backs and gaze upwards.

We can look up through the shimmering leaves of a tree in full leaf or past the samphire and jagged rocks of a Devon cliff to the wheeling birds and the clouds above, and wonder whether high cirrus will bring wind before long or whether cumulus will deteriorate into cumulo-nimbus to bring a deluge.

We can speculate on how far our great landscape painters captured actuality and how far they were trying with visual images to hint of a greater reality, and a dimension of existence beyond what is immediately apparent to the senses. That sensation of something beyond what our eyes take in is not nearly as uncommon as some people might think.

We can recall that it has been said that all art aspires to the condition of music and remember the more obvious examples of music that conjure up the natural world, such as the storm in Beethoven's *Pastoral* Symphony, the Impressionist mood music of Debussy or the altogether more violent Stravinsky's *Rite of Spring*.

We may remember that without the English countryside, nobody would have written *On hearing the first Cuckoo in Spring*, or *The Lark Ascending*. Nor would we have our rich legacy of haunting, sad or jaunty folk songs – so many of which spring from life in the countryside. The old singers would not have been able to walk out on May mornings or seen the dew blown away.

Even after two world wars there was plenty of peaceful countryside left in Britain to help heal the emotional wounds from which returning heroes and their families suffered. Now much of it has vanished under brick and concrete: yet more of it may succumb to road-building and urban sprawl. The need to save what is left is not an idle whim of armchair aesthetes. It is an imperative for all who have eyes to see and ears to hear. If it is disregarded because of short-term economics and the demands of the roads lobby, increased social unrest, worse pollution and continued loss of quality of life will be the inevitable result. Is that the kind of Britain our leaders really want?

TIM WILLIAMS

NORTHAM

Of course, we LIKE growing. There is something intrinsically pleasing about raising a perfect cauliflower from a seed no bigger than a speck of pepper or creating twenty new plants from a tangled mass of roots.

There is an aesthetic beauty – rows of crops with different leaf shapes, height and growing cycles forming a huge collage which changes every minute of every day – as the crops grow larger and larger and are harvested – creating gaps – the light changes according to the time of day, season, weather. There is another influence on our tapestry – one that we impose on it – we grow our crops in strict rotation – it will be five years before the same crop is grown again on any particular patch.

It is perhaps easier, at first glance, to appreciate this beauty in the ornamental garden, where there are the additional attractions of flower colour and scent. There is something in flower here, somewhere, from January to November and the shrubs provide an interest with the colours and form of their foliage and bark, but the permanence of the planting lacks the fluidity of the vegetable fields.

During our cultivations of the soil we find a wide variety of insects and small mammals, both outside and in the protected areas. Some of the insects, in their varying stages of life, are difficult to identify as there are such a infinitely baffling array of them, but each one has its place, be it friend or foe and we are hesitant to destroy the natural balance.

There is nothing quite like the taste of freshly harvested vegetables. We have a horror of modern food production methods and the effects on wildlife. Habitats have been irrevocably destroyed – hedgerows torn out, trees felled, water courses polluted by excess nitrogen – in the drive for ever increased productivity. The long term effects of pesticide use on food chains are still unknown. We would wish our children to enjoy the wealth of species that the countryside has.

The nursery is now an entity in its own right – like a giant machine – ever turning with the relentless passing of the seasons and always with something more to be done. It imposes its own discipline in the timing of the processes, to make order from the turmoil of different crops and conditions, which in turn feeds the motivation that we find from deep within ourselves.

And yet it is still changing. We have a continuing quest to develop the nursery as one integrated unit – to use and re-use our own water, to harness the energy of the wind and the sun. With the trail that we have established (with ELMS support) our visitors can observe our approach and perhaps take something of that home with them. The past nine seasons have an influence on the future – we have changed and evolved with the land.

David and Vanessa Ebdon

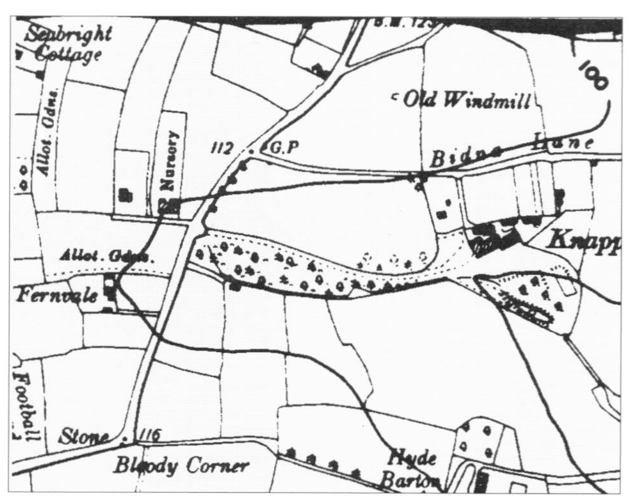
Sebright Cottage
Old Windmill
100
Allot. Gdns.
Nursery
112
G.P
Allot. Gdns.
Fernvale
Football
Stone
116
Bloody Corner
Hyde Barton

Gardening is an occupation pleasing in itself, because it gives one those cheerful feelings of high health, which always arise from exercise; and because one has always the satisfaction of finding the plot, the path, or the border, visibly bettered by the shorter labour; and the growth of the plants, the unfolding of blossoms, and the keeping of fruit, all our own, give us lasting gratification, which is varied and increased as they assume their shape and colour in growing to perfection: and there is such a numerous succession of flowers and vegetables, from the snow drop that blooms and dies in the cold winds of February, to the gigantic rosemallow of August; and from the fair young potato – the untimely fruit of the spring – to the scarlet blossomed tendril of the late French bean; that the attention is never weary, and the appetite never cloyed. But there are other gratifications in this pleasing occupation. For though the gardener knows that the smallest blade of grass is nothing less than a stupendous work of omnipotence, he yet finds that the growth of plants is regulated and perfected by his skill and attention; so that when he receives the fruits of the soil he has tilled, he proudly identifies his labour in the creation of them. And how much sweeter do things seem when they are the long-known productions of one's own soil, than when we buy them from strange hands! and how pleasing it is to know that, whether one prefers the red and juicy radish, or the cucumber that stretches its tough and bulky body on the warm earth, or whether one wishes for the crooked pear or the yellow apricot; all are within one's reach! and all one's own!

EXTRACTS FROM *GARDENING*
WILLIAM BARNES

Nature will not tolerate stagnation. All is birth and growth and efflorescence, and every new green shoot is a denial of death.

In the Winter the earth appears to be a barren waste, a vast cemetery filled with dead and decaying substances; yet in reality it is a great womb of dormant life, full of bulbs and roots and seeds. At the appointed moment, something wakes them into activity, and down in the dark clay chambers of the soil secret processes of growth are set into operation, and the earth which had been masked with the appearance of Death breaks out into a living glory of leaf and bloom.

Hidden lines of communication are opened up and the mysterious message flashes from bulb to bulb and root to root.

All Nature bids us hope and be glad in the hoping, for Spring is the eternal demonstration of resurrection and renewal.

PATIENCE STRONG

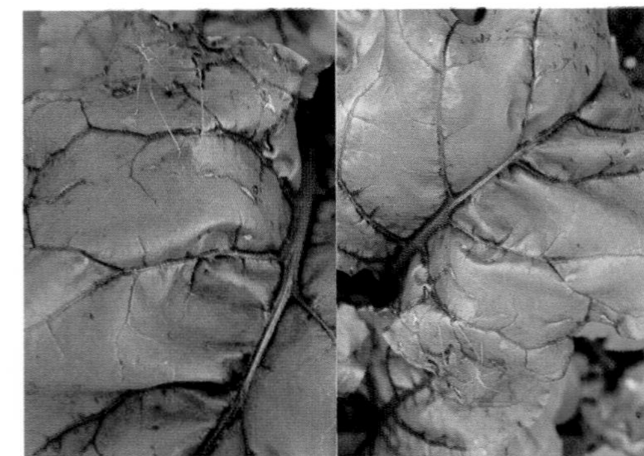

I thought on the fruit and plants
that were ripening around me,
I exclaimed to myself,
'O fortunatos, sua si bena norint,
Agricolas!'
How happy, if they know their bliss,
are they who till
the ground.

WILLIAM BARNES

BABELEIGH BARTON

The area of twenty acres that comprises the ELMS site at Babeleigh Barton was presumably farmed as two fields up to the mid 1800s. These were named as Far Wenter Marsh and Rear Wenter Marsh. They were probably allowed to degenerate back to their original wild state in the farming depression of the pre First World War period.

The area is a mixture of marshy culm grassland surrounded by trees on the original hedges and mixed scrub on the fringes. It contains many unusual wetland species and is home to a wide variety of wildlife including roe deer and migratory birds in winter.

My father came to Babeleigh in 1940 and on his death in 1982, due to the normal demands of family wills and inheritance tax,the farm had to be geared commercially at a much higher level. Subsequently I had to consider reclaiming as much land as possible albeit reluctantly as I have always enjoyed the wild areas of the farm.

It was then that I read about the ELMS scheme and contacted the Devon FWAG officer who inspected the site and helped me submit an application which was obviously successful. The net result is that I have been able to retain a beautiful area of wetland in its natural state, enjoyed by the wildlife, myself and any other interested parties. This is a tribute to the imagination and foresight of the people who set up the above scheme on behalf of Devon County Council.

JOHN TUCKER

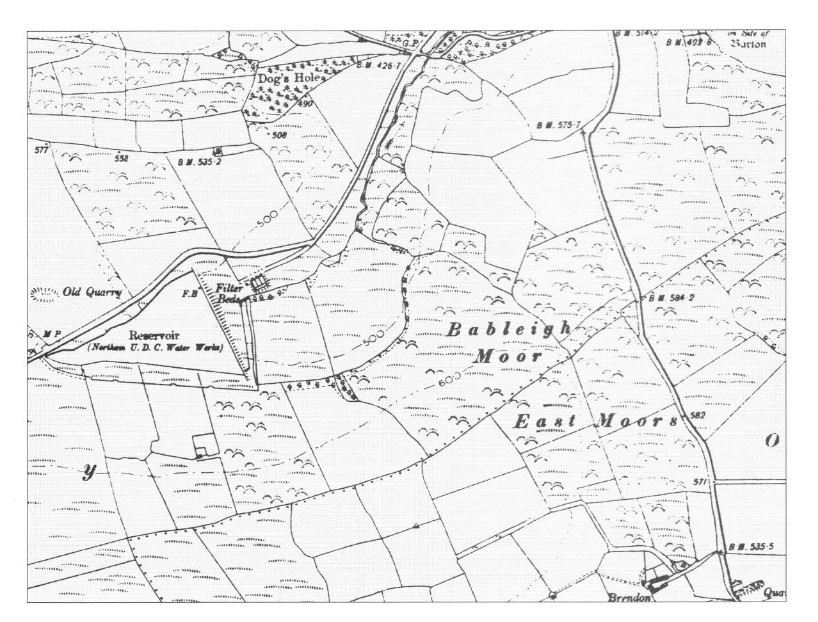

Dog's Hole
B.M. 426·7
B.M. 575·7
B.M. 535·2
Old Quarry
F.B
Filter Beds
Reservoir
(Northam U.D.C. Water Works)
Bableigh Moor
East Moors
B.M. 584·2
B.M. 535·5
Brendon
Barton

Seek out a wood, and draw serenity from the silent trees.
In the green days of summer or the grey days of winter,
the hush of the woodlands falls like a benediction
upon the tired spirit

Stand very still, and listen to the silence.
It is more eloquent than the most inspiring preacher:
Its meaning holds a deeper beauty
than the greatest poem that has ever been written.

PATIENCE STRONG